D0296840

WITHD...
THE LIBRARY

UNIVERSITY OF
WINCHESTER

AUTHOR BOARDMAN

TITLE Greek art

ACCESSION No. 20769

KA 0123054 9

Greek Art

1 Athenian Geometric *amphora* with encircling bands of Geometric patterns interrupted by rows of grazing deer, recumbent goats and geese. *c.* 750 B.C. Height 16¼ ins

GREEK ART

JOHN BOARDMAN

THAMES AND HUDSON · LONDON

KING ALFRED'S COLLEGE
LIBRARY.

© THAMES AND HUDSON 1964
PRINTED IN GREAT BRITAIN BY JARROLD AND SONS LTD, NORWICH

Contents

Page 9 Introduction

21 CHAPTER ONE
The Beginnings and Geometric Greece

41 CHAPTER TWO
Greece and the Arts of the East and Egypt

67 CHAPTER THREE
Archaic Greek Art

119 CHAPTER FOUR
Classical Sculpture and Architecture

161 CHAPTER FIVE
Other Arts in Classical Greece

203 CHAPTER SIX
Hellenistic Art

253 CHAPTER SEVEN
Epilogue

268 Chronological Chart

271 Selected Bibliography

273 List of Illustrations

282 Index

THE GREEK WORLD

Olbia

Danube

Istros

BLACK SEA

Sinope

Trapezus

ACE

Bosphorus

Byzantium

Perinthus

Chalcedon

Heraclea

Halys

Sea of
Marmara

Cyzicus

Gordion

TROAD

PHRYGIA

AEOLIS

Pergamum

sbos

Cyme

Phocaea

LYDIA

Tigris

ios

Smyrna

Sardis

IONIA

Maeander

Karatepe

Ephesus

mos

Priene

CARIA

CILICIA

Tarsus

Miletus

Perge

Euphrates

Halicarnassus

Antioch

Cos

LYCIA

Cnidus

Phaselis

Al Mina

Orontes

Lindos

Xanthos

SYRIA

RHODES

CYPRUS

Praesus

Citium

Salamis

RETE

Paphos

Byblos

PHOENICIA

NEAN

Sidon

Tyre

Jerusalem

PALESTINE

Jericho

Alexandria

Naucratis

Memphis

Nile

RED SEA

Introduction

'Some girls affect what is called the Grecian bend' commented the *Daily Telegraph* in 1869, and the Irish ballad applauds the 'sort of creature, boys, that nature did intend, to walk right through the world' without that affectation. It is a measure of the popular view of Greek art and of ancient Greeks in general that 'Grecian bend' was coined for the affected gait, leaning forward from the hips, seen in nineteenth-century England. It is hard to see just what Classical poses inspired the term, but it became current soon after the arrival in England of the Elgin Marbles. They had recently been rescued from the Acropolis in Athens and offered English artists and scholars their first opportunity to appreciate a large complex of original Greek statuary of the finest period. It need hardly be said that there were many dissenters who preferred still the slick prettiness of Classical artists like Canova (who himself appreciated the Elgin Marbles: 'Oh! that I had but to begin again') and derived their notion of Greek art from them. The notion dies hard too, together with other misconceptions about ancient Greece. The 'Greek profiles' of actors of the silent film were admired, and even Schliemann expressed naïve surprise when he excavated the skeletons of the Greeks who died at the Battle of Chaeronea and saw that they had not got 'Classical' noses. Isadora Duncan dancing on the steps of the Parthenon would have looked far odder to the ancient Athenian than the chorus of *West Side Story*. The grammar of Greek architecture is now readily understood, however transmuted, for we see it dimly still in all sorts of construction—from the façades of banks to the dentils incongruously crowning a pillar-box. And we even find straight copies, like the Caryatid porch of the Erechtheion in Athens on the Church of St Pancras, in London.

This popular view of Greek art is so commonplace and the truth so subtly different, that it is worth while considering for a moment how we have come to know the art of the ancient Greeks. We have also to distinguish it from that of Roman copyists and the Renaissance, for these are the intermediaries who cherished the Classical tradition in Western art.

Some monuments of Greek antiquity remained visible in Italy and Sicily in the Greek colonial sites, but Italian scholars and artists were naturally first attracted to Roman remains, the clay relief bowls (Arretine) and coins being collected already in the thirteenth and fourteenth centuries. In the fifteenth century some of the big Italian collections of sculpture were being formed, and not only from finds in Italy, for scholars were visiting Greek lands and both Venetian and Genoese families were trading freely in the Aegean. The young Michelangelo was proud that his work could be mistaken for antique, and artists like Piranesi ran studios in which incomplete statues, like the pieces from Hadrian's Villa at Tivoli, were repaired and completed.

2 Marble lion before the Arsenal at Venice. The body is from Delos, of the late seventh century B.C.; the head is an eighteenth-century A.D. addition

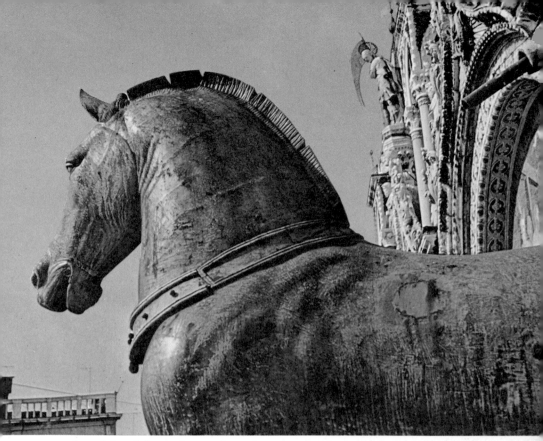

3 One of the gilt bronze horses, above the entrance to St Mark's, Venice. Original Greek works of the Hellenistic period which once stood on the island of Chios

Even earlier some Greek work had reached Italy. The great gilt bronze horses (*Ill. 3*) which today stand over the entrance to St Mark's, Venice, had been taken to the Hippodrome of Constantinople from Chios in the fifth century A.D., and thence to Venice, as part of the Crusader booty, in 1204. There they were threatened with being melted down in the Arsenal, but the poet Petrarch and others recognized their value and beauty: 'Works of Lysippus himself', they said, and they were probably made not much after the lifetime of that sculptor. To Venetians they showed the brilliant casting techniques of the ancients, forgotten again until Donatello. The prizes

11

have not stood undisturbed on St Mark's. Napoleon took them to Paris in 1798 and mounted them on the Arc du Carrousel in the Tuileries. They were returned in 1815, despite the popular outcry for their retention. And in the First World War they came down again under the threat of Austrian bombardment. The two lions before Venice Arsenal also came from Greece: one from Piraeus, port of Athens, the other a fine Archaic creature from Delos, which was brought in the early eighteenth century and had to be provided with a new head in the contemporary manner (*Ill. 2*).

The big Italian collections remain an important source for the study of Greek statuary—in Roman copies—although the cult of the fig leaf persists here and there, and the copy of Praxiteles's Aphrodite in the Vatican only lost the lead drapery swathed decently round her hips in 1932. Similar collections grew in France, where Louis XIV's sculptor, Girardon, was called upon to perform an early instance of plastic surgery on the Venus of Arles (another Praxitelean copy) to reduce her pose, dress, and the contour of her breasts to something nearer the contemporary fashion. In England the Earl of Arundel (*Ill. 4*), much of whose collection is in Oxford, had travelled in

4 The Earl of Arundel (1585–1646) in his sculpture gallery at Arundel House, London. Painted by Mytens. The Earl had visited Italy in the company of the architect, Inigo Jones and sponsored excavations there. Later he collected marbles from the Aegean area and his gallery was visited and admired by Rubens. Canvas, 81½ × 50 ins

5 The Temporary Elgin Room in the British Museum in 1819. A painting by
A. Archer. Canvas, 38 × 54 ins

Greece and was able to acquire several important Greek originals in
the early seventeenth century. One piece from his collection, now
recognized as from the Great Altar of Zeus at Pergamum, wandered
as far as Worksop, where it was built into the front of a Georgian red-
brick house and refused by a firm of masons for breaking into chips
before it was rescued and recognized in 1961.

But it was the really big finds of the late eighteenth and early
nineteenth century that opened the eyes of Western Europe to
original Greek art. The sculptures of the Temple of Aphaea at
Aegina went to Munich. Elgin's Marbles from Athens were acquired
for the British Museum in 1816, and despite the condition of
exhibition (*Ill.* 5) and some strong expression of prejudice, came to
be valued at their true worth, and had a profound influence on

13

6 The staircase in the Ashmolean Museum, Oxford, with a restored and partly coloured cast of the frieze from the fifth-century B.C. Temple of Apollo at Bassae (see *Ills. 126–8*). Designed by C. R. Cockerell, 1845

artists, and on the more popular and scholarly ideas about Greece. C. R. Cockerell explored and drew the Temple of Apollo at Bassae, and its relief sculptures too came to London (see *Ills. 126–8*). When he built the University Galleries at Oxford (now the Ashmolean Museum) in 1845 he recalled the unusual column types of Bassae in the exterior, and at the top of the staircase (*Ill. 6*) set a cast of the sculpture frieze from the inner room of the temple, where, with its painted background and in an architectural setting, it can give some idea of the part such architectural sculpture can play in decoration. Even the Great Exhibition of 1851 had its tribute to antiquity, although when the historian of Greece, George Finlay, visited it with 'Athenian' Penrose, who had studied and elucidated the architectural refinements of the Parthenon itself, he wrote afterwards in his diary, 'Crystal Palace with Penrose. The frieze of the Parthenon is fearful coloured and the Egyptian figures not only men but lions and sphinxes look as if they were drunk.'

Greek vases were being found in quantity in the cemeteries of Etruria and South Italy from the eighteenth century on. At first

14

called Etruscan, their Greek character was eventually recognized, although the earlier vases of Greece, when they first appeared in Greek lands, were dismissed as Phoenician or Egyptian, so unlike were they to the Classical statues and vase paintings. Greek and Roman gems had remained in use as decoration through the Middle Ages, and had been copied freely. The nineteenth-century excavations in Greece itself revealed new treasures, both of major statuary like the Olympia sculptures and the Archaic marbles of the Athenian Acropolis, and the host of other works on which scholars can now

7 Copy of a relief showing Hermes, Orpheus and Eurydice; one of the four from the Altar of the Twelve Gods set up in the Athenian marketplace in the later fifth century B.C.

8 The head of a bronze *kouros*, fresh from its discovery in the Piraeus, port of
Athens, in 1959. Lifesize

base a reasoned history of the whole development of Greek art, the summary of which is attempted in these chapters.

The problems which attend the understanding of the history of Greek art are no fewer now that so much more evidence is available, but they have reached the point at which discussion can concern matters of attribution to individual artists, rather than the broader considerations of date. There is still much to be gleaned from the accounts of ancient authors, in the identification of famous Greek works in copies of the Roman period, and, for example, in the identification of portraits. Some results come from a happy combination of excavation, observation and brilliant detective work. A good example is the demonstration that the originals of a well-known series of four reliefs (*Ill. 7*), known in several late copies, stood in the balustrade around the Altar of the Twelve Gods in the marketplace of Classical Athens.

New excavations provide both new works of art and fresh evidence for the understanding and dating of works already known. Not all the finds are quite deliberate. Wrecked ships carrying statues, probably *en route* for Roman palaces or villas, have yielded some of the finest major bronzes of the Classical period. The Roman General Sulla sacked the port of Piraeus in 86 B.C., and seems to have surprised a shipment of statuary which never got away but was burned in its warehouse. The statues were rediscovered in 1959 while a sewer was being dug in the streets of Piraeus (*Ill. 8*). It might well be thought that the major sites likely to yield notable works have by now been all discovered and exhausted. This seems far from true. In the first place there are the many unexpected finds far from Greece which sometimes produce works unrivalled in Greece itself: I think of the tomb at Vix, little over one hundred miles south-east of Paris, which in 1953 yielded the largest and finest of all Archaic bronze *craters* yet known; or Panagurishte in Bulgaria where in 1949 a spectacular hoard of Hellenistic gold vases was uncovered (see *Ill. 220*). There are new sites in Greece too, like the Classical sanctuary at Brauron in Attica and the Hellenistic palaces of North Greece. Meanwhile the old sites are far from exhausted and the lower levels of great sites like Delphi and the Heraion on Samos still surprise us with their treasures.

At Olympia it was too late by nearly two millennia to rescue the gold and ivory statue of Zeus, made by Phidias, and one of the seven wonders of the Ancient World. But in 1954–8 Phidias's workshop, in which the statue was made, was excavated, with its tools, scraps of ivory, moulds for the glass inlays and matrices on which the sheet-gold was beaten out; and in the corner the great artist's own tea-mug with his name incised on the base, 'I belong to Phidias' (*Ill. 9*). These finds may not take us much closer to the great statue, but they teach us a lot about how it was made, as well as offering a rather poignant relic of the greatest of all Classical artists.

The perplexity with which scholars faced the evidence of those works of Greek art which are earlier than the Classical has already been remarked. Certainly, a Geometric vase is as different as it can be from a red-figure one, and there is little in seventh-century sculpture to suggest that within two centuries Greek artists were to carve statuary of the quality and type which appeared on the Parthenon. In a way this is the most remarkable lesson of any history of Greek art—its rapid but deliberate development from strict geometry admitting hardly any figure decoration, to full realism of anatomy and expression. We shall see how the geometry broke before the influence of Near Eastern art, and how the Greek artists absorbed these foreign elements and welded them into an art form in which the best formal qualities of their native tradition remained dominant. And then, at about the time of the Persian Wars, a break with conventions and a steady progress, centred in the study of representation of the human body, towards the unrivalled competence of the fourth century and Hellenistic Greece.

When we have to contrast one style with another and we use words like 'the Archaic' and 'the Classical', 'the Geometric' and 'the Orientalizing', this is simply a matter of convenient terminology, for the development from one style to another is smooth, only accelerated by outside influence or the brilliance of particular schools. And, of course, it is easy to fall into errors of talking about the 'sixth-century style'—another sheer convenience—utterly meaning-less, of course, to the ancients who did not know what century B.C. they were living in, although they could readily recognize what was

9 Base of an Athenian black cup with graffito, bearing the signature of the sculptor Phidias, found in the studio at Olympia where he made the cult statue of Zeus

primitive in their own art. We can talk with only a little more conviction about the different spirit of Quattrocento and Cinquecento Italy. The passage into a new century or decade in modern times is more readily felt to be significant in some way: 'the nineties', 'the twenties' are to a fair degree valid individual periods.

Finally, the pictures in this book. The finest vase-painting styles are essentially linear, black-and-white (or rather red). Greek sculpture was coloured, but the colour has seldom lasted even in slight traces. There were fine wall paintings, but none have survived, except in late copies. So if in picture-books Greek art looks colourless beside, say, Egyptian, or the arts of more recent periods, we must make allowances for the problems of survival. In these chapters the theme is one of change and development, with an emphasis on the less well-known arts which are too readily forgotten, and special emphasis on original works rather than copies. Histories of art tend to be written around the few stock masterpieces. It is well to realize how much more there is and the fulness of the evidence. In choosing the pictures no conscious effort has been made to include all the old favourites, any more than to seek out the unknown deliberately. To omit a picture of the Delphi charioteer from such a book is no more serious than to omit a host of other equally or more important, though less popular, works.

CHAPTER ONE

The Beginnings and Geometric Greece

There is no difficulty in tracing the development of the Classical tradition in Western art from Greece of the fifth century B.C., through Rome, the Renaissance, to the modern world. Working backwards, to its origins, the story is no less clear, but it is extraordinarily varied and there are two views about what should be regarded as its starting-point. Once the Geometric art of Greece was recognized for what it was, the steps by which it was linked to the Classical period were quickly traced. This was the work of scholars of the end of the nineteenth century, who were at last able to show that Classical art was not a sudden apparition, like Athena springing fully armed from the head of Zeus, nor a brilliant amalgam of the arts of Assyria and Egypt, but independently evolved by Greeks in Greece, and its course only superficially conditioned by the influence and instruction of other cultures.

But even while the importance of Geometric Greece was being recognized, excavators like Schliemann and Evans were probing deeper into Greece's past. The arts of Minoan Crete and of Mycenae had to be added to the sum of the achievements of peoples in Greek lands, and now that it has been proved that the Mycenaeans were themselves Greek-speakers the question naturally arises whether the origins of Classical Greek art are not to be sought yet further back, in the centuries which saw the supremacy of the Mycenaean Empire.

The trouble has been to find a link across the Dark Ages which followed the violent overthrow of the Mycenaean world in the twelfth century B.C. It would be idle to pretend that there is none, but the fact remains that Mycenaean art, which is itself but a provincial version of the arts of the non-Greek Minoans, is utterly different, both at first sight and in most of its principles, to that of Geometric Greece. For this reason our story begins after the Dark Ages, with Greek artists working out afresh, and without the overwhelming incubus of the Minoan tradition to stifle them, art forms which satisfied their peculiar temperament, and out of which the Classical tradition was born.

For this reason our only picture of Bronze Age, Mycenaean Greece here is probably the most familiar one—the Lion Gate at the main entrance to the castle at Mycenae (*Ill. 10*). There is more, however, than its familiarity which suggests its inclusion. It was one of the few monuments of Mycenaean Greece which must have remained visible to Greeks in the Classical period, beside massive walls which they attributed to the work of giants. And it illustrates two features of Mycenaean art which were not learnt from the Minoans, and which the Minoans had never appreciated. First, the monumental quality of the architecture, massive blocks and lintels piled fearlessly to make the stout castle walls which the life of Mycenaean royalty found necessary. Secondly, the monumental quality of the statuary, impressive here for its sheer size rather than anything else, since the art form derived directly from the Minoan tradition which was essentially miniaturist and decorative. More than five hundred years were to pass before Greek sculptors could command an idiom which would satisfy these aspirations in sculpture and architecture.

The revival, or rather the rebirth of Greek art after the fall of the Mycenaean world introduces a city which seems to have had slight importance in the Bronze Age, but which is to dominate the story from now on—Athens. To some degree the Acropolis citadel of Athens had survived the disasters attendant on the destruction of other Mycenaean centres, and her countryside was to serve as a refuge for other Greeks dispossessed by the invaders from the north. It is on painted clay vases that we can best observe the change that takes place, and since about one-quarter of the pictures illustrating this book will be of decorated pottery—nowadays a somewhat recherché art form—it will be as well to explain why this is. Virtually all that we know about the art of these early centuries has been won from the soil, and the rigours of survival have determined what our evidence shall be. No textiles, embroidery or woodwork, for one thing. Only by good fortune marble or bronze statuary, since the materials were only too readily appreciated by later generations as

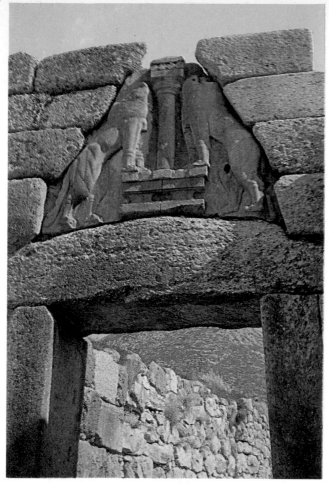

10 The Lion Gate at Mycenae. Two lions, their heads missing, stand heraldically at either side of an altar supporting a column. The triangular slab helps to relieve the weight of masonry on the great lintel. Thirteenth century B.C.

raw material for their lime-kilns or furnaces. But a fired-clay vase, with its painted decoration fired hard upon it, is almost indestructible. It can be broken, of course, but short of grinding the pieces to powder something will remain. In an age in which metal was expensive, and glass, cardboard and plastics unknown, clay vessels served more purposes than they do today, and in Greece at least the artist found on them a suitable field for the exercise of his draughts-manship.

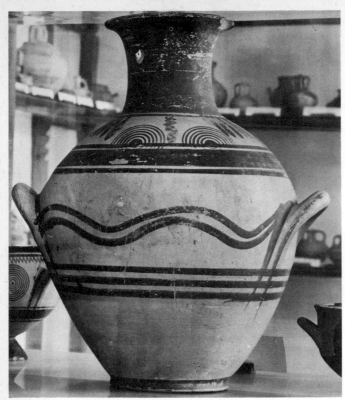

11 A Protogeometric *amphora* from Athens, with the characteristic concentric semicircles on the neck, and wavy line at the belly. Vases of this shape, with belly handles, were used for women's graves. Early tenth century B.C. Height 16⁵⁄₁₆ ins

On the vases made in Athens in the tenth century B.C., we see the simplest of the Mycenaean patterns, arcs and circles, translated into a new decorative form by the use of compasses and multiple comb-like brushes which rendered with a sharp precision the loosely hand-drawn patterns of the older style (*Ill. 11*). A few other simple Geometric patterns are admitted, but because we have yet to reach the full Geometric style of Greece, this period is called Protogeometric. The vases themselves are better made, better proportioned, and the painted decoration on neck or belly is skilfully suited to the simple, effective shape. The painters had not forgotten how to produce the fine black gloss paint of the best Bronze Age vases, and as the Proto-geometric style developed we see more of the surface of the vase covered by the black paint.

The vases that we have come mostly from tombs and there is little enough to set beside them, except for simple bronze safety-pins (*fibulae*) and some primitive clay figures, especially from Crete

24

(*Ill. 12*) where, again, some of the Minoan forms and techniques seem to have survived. Of the domestic architecture and temples we know nothing, and have no reason to believe that they were anything more than the very simplest constructions—of rubble or mud brick. This was true of all parts of Greece at this time, and the Protogeometric style of Athens' pottery was soon accepted as the standard for vase decoration far from its place of origin. But this cannot mean that Athens enjoyed also any sort of political supremacy in a Greece of small independent cities and kingdoms.

GEOMETRIC VASES

The full Geometric period belongs to the ninth and eighth centuries B.C. It begins, or rather slowly develops from the relative obscurity of the Protogeometric, and ends with a new, prosperous Greece of strong city-states, whose merchants and families were already travelling far from the home waters of the Aegean to trade and settle and whose nobles were already looking for something of the luxury and the trappings of Court life as it was known in the older civilizations of the Near East and Egypt, and as it had been known in Greece's own Golden Age of Heroes, the Bronze Age.

12 A janiform clay head from Crete, which may have fitted into a roughly carved wooden body and served as a cult idol. The two faces (one male—at the back, one female?) were painted. Tenth–ninth century B.C. $11\frac{1}{2}$ $\times 7\frac{1}{2}$ ins

13 An Athenian Geometric *crater* with meander, zigzags and early representations of horses. The knob of the lid is finished as a small jug. *c.* 800 B.C. Height 22 $\frac{7}{16}$ ins; diam. between handles 10 $\frac{3}{16}$ ins

On the Geometric vases we soon begin to see a new repertory of patterns as well as the decorative development of the old ones. The vases are girt by continuous bands of meanders, zigzags and triangles, to name only the most popular patterns (*Ill. 13*). The circles and semicircles are seen less often. These zones are divided from each other by neat triple lines, and the patterns themselves are drawn in outline and hatched. Much of this is strongly reminiscent of ordinary basketry designs, and while it is clear that there was some influence from this craft, even in some vase shapes (*pyxides* like knitting-baskets) it still does not explain the whole phenomenon of Geometric decoration. Several new vase shapes are introduced, as well as refinements of the old, to suit the more varied needs of a more prosperous and sophisticated community.

While in the Protogeometric period the artist confined his decoration to clearly defined areas of the vase, the Geometric painter soon let zones of zigzags and meanders cover the whole vessel, filling in the blank spaces of the earlier vases with strips of simple pattern. The overall effect is fussy, but precise, and the shape is still well enough expressed by setting the emphatic patterns at the neck, shoulder or between the handles. But it looks as though the artist soon became absorbed with the patterns themselves, and variants upon them, to the detriment of the general effect of the vase as an expression of the wedded crafts of potter and painter. The zones are broken into panels with individual motifs of circles, swastikas or diamonds, and the resultant checkered appearance has a depressingly rhythmic effect.

However, at the time that these changes were being made, in the early eighth century, the artist also began to admit figure decoration to his vases. At first only animals—horses, deer, fowl—one animal in one pose repeated exactly to fill a frieze where before a meander or zigzag ran (*Ill. 1*). And the effect is still of a Geometric frieze, with the grazing or reclining animals presenting a repetitive pattern of limbs and bodies, rather than individual studies. By the mid-century human figures were admitted too in scenes of some complexity. The finest appear in the main panels on the big funeral vases which stood (some over five feet high) marking graves in an Athens cemetery

14 This large *crater* (mixing-bowl) stood over a man's grave in Athens. The base was pierced so that libations poured into the vase reached the burial. The main scene shows the funeral bier on a cart, being taken to burial with rows of mourners and, beneath, chariots with warriors carrying *Dipylon* shields. *c.* 750 B.C. Height 48 ins

(*Ill. 14*). Here we can best observe the way the artist treated his figure studies. It was an idiom which sprang from the discipline of the Geometric patterns, which were all he knew, and it owes nothing to the influence or example of other cultures, although broadly similar conventions have been adopted in different parts of the world at different times. The parts of the body are rendered in angular sticks and triangles, blobs for the heads, bulging sausage-like thighs and calves. The whole figure is thus reduced to a Geometric pattern (*Ill. 15*). All is rendered in plain silhouette and only later is an eye reserved within the head, and strands of hair are shown, as well as chins, noses, fingers and breasts. The artist paints what he knows of the figures, not what he sees, and though he did not show both eyes in a profile head, still, in chariot groups, all legs, tails and necks of all four horses would be shown, and the two wheels put side by side. On the funeral bier the checkered shroud, lifted over the corpse, is cut away to show clearly the body beneath. Action, like fighting, is shown easily enough with these stick figures and their spears, swords and bows; and emotion is translated into action—like the mourners tearing their hair. On the grave vases we see the body laid out for burial (*prothesis*), or the bier carried by carts to the cemetery (*ekphora*): the centrepiece flanked by rows of mourners so that the whole still forms a symmetrical, Geometric composition, although it is also telling a story. Sea fights are shown on some vases, and although, from their quaint equipment, it seems likely that the artists thought of their figures as heroes of the past, still the sort of actions in which they were involved may have been taken from contemporary life.

15 Detail from the vase shown in *Ill. 14.* The mourning women (breasts shown by strokes at either side of the triangle torsos) tear their hair. The charioteers' helmets are reduced to a crest only, but of their chariots we see both wheels and rails, and of their horses all legs, tails and necks

On the smaller vases too these figure scenes become more and more common. Here we are offered the earliest and clearest expression of that interest in narrative art which is an essential part of the Classical tradition. In literature it is expressed first in the Homeric Poems, and it is no accident that it is just at this time that Homer must have been moulding the lays about the Age of Heroes into the epic poems from which artists—poets, dramatists, sculptors and painters—were to draw inspiration for centuries to come. Some of the protagonists on the vase scenes may be identified as heroes of popular Greek myths in characteristic exploits—like Heracles's encounter with the lion. Others may illustrate heroic episodes—duels at Troy, the shipwreck of Odysseus, or Nestor with the twins Molione. Others present sketches of everyday life—dances, boxing-matches, the chase (*Ill. 16*). Only at the end of the Geometric period do we see the drawing of the rigid silhouette loosened and new creatures, like the lion, faced by a hero, tearing a warrior or hunting. The appearance of this beast heralds a new age (*Ills. 16, 17*).

16 Athenian Late Geometric drinking-cup (*kantharos*) showing, in the main frieze, a warrior leading away a woman, a duel, two lions tearing a warrior, and a lyre-player talking to two water-girls. Late eighth century B.C. Height 6⅜ ins

17 An Athenian Late Geometric *amphora* from Attica. The Geometric ornament is now wholly subordinated to figure scenes: a lion pulling down a doe, grazing horses and chariots shown in a reasonable profile view. Reserved areas admit details of eyes and manes. *c.* 700 B.C. Height 24¼ ins

18 Late Geometric vase from the island of Thera, where this style, with broad plain bands on the body, seems especially at home. Late eighth century B.C. Height 28¾ ins

The other Greek cities followed Athens' lead in Geometric vase decoration, as they had in the preceding period, but there is less slavish imitation now and several distinct, if not always very distinguished local schools of Late Geometric vase painting can be picked out. None seems to have attempted the elaborate narrative scenes such as appear in Athens, but Argos (in the Peloponnese) and Boeotia (in Central Greece) had figure scenes on vases charged with variants of the usual Geometric patterns, and there were good local schools in Crete and the islands (*Ill. 18*). In the next chapter we shall see what replaced the Geometric decoration on pottery, but it is worth remembering that the patterns long remained popular, and that the basic, architectonic, principle of Geometric decoration was never forgotten; indeed it is one of the underlying factors in Greek art of all periods.

OTHER ARTS

The figure style of the Geometric vases reappears on the many other objects, of other materials, which were being made in the eighth century B.C. We know about these from the richer gifts which now accompany burials, and from their appearance as offerings

19 Decorative bronze safety-pin (*fibula*), its pin missing, of a type made in Boeotia around 700 B.C. One side of the catch-plate shows a duel between bowmen above a ship; the other a hero fighting the Siamese twins, Molione. Length 8¼ ins

20 Late Geometric stone seal showing a centaur (man-horse) attacked by a bowman, possibly Heracles. Compare the figures drawn on vases, as *Ill. 16*

in sanctuaries—both the national sanctuaries like Delphi and Olympia which attracted dedications from all over the Greek world and sometimes outside it, and the local shrines.

Figures like the more elaborate painted examples are found incised on the flat catch-plates or bows of safety-pin *fibulae* made in Athens and Boeotia towards the end of our period (*Ill. 19*). There are simpler ones impressed on the gold bands which are found on the heads of the dead, as well as more advanced animal studies which anticipate the new style. Another early intimation of the influence of the Near East is the resumption of seal engraving in Greece. The earliest seals, made in the islands, are square blocks of limestone, but the designs on them are wholly Geometric and not Eastern in spirit (*Ill. 20*).

When we come to bronze figures in the round the picture is somewhat different. On the one hand we have some rather stylish figures of horses and stags, which, although they are cast in the round, strongly resemble the cut-out or flat hammered figurines from which they probably derive. Occasionally more elaborate groups are composed of such figures—mares or deer with their young (*Ill. 21*), a centaur-like monster fighting a god. Other bronze figurines, cast solid from an individual mould, are rendered in a much freer, plastic style and reflect the easy modelling of the soft clay or wax from which their moulds were made. Still, their broad shoulders and elongated bodies broadly match painted figures on vases (*Ill. 23*). The bronzes are generally of naked men, perhaps intended to represent a god—Zeus at Olympia—and may be equipped with helmet, spear and shield. Rarely we find groups, like the lion-hunt (*Ill. 22*), or action figures, like a helmet-maker squatting at his work, or a charioteer. In the lion-hunt from Samos the artist has given the monster (which he has never seen) elephantine legs, but appropriately massive jaws and shoulders. Many figurines of men and horses were intended as decorative attachments to the rims of bronze cauldrons (*Ill. 24*). These magnificent vessels were valuable offerings standing

34

21 Bronze group of a deer with a fawn, the bodies decorated with groups of circles. A bird is perched on the deer's rump. Late eighth century B.C. Height 2¾ ins

22 Bronze group showing a hunter and his dog attacking a lion, its prey in its mouth. The hunter wears a helmet and is perhaps a hero. The group is from Samos. Late eighth century B.C.

23 Bronze warrior from Karditsa in North Greece. His spear is missing but he wears a heroic *Dipylon* shield at his back; otherwise only a belt and cap-helmet. *c.* 700 B.C. Height 11 ins

24 (*left*) Bronze figure, from the rim of a bronze cauldron dedicated at Olympia soon after 700 B.C. With a companion he would have supported an upright ring handle. Height 14½ ins

25 (*right*) Clay figure of a woman. The legs were made separately and suspended inside. The painted decoration resembles that on vases and shows a line of women dancing. Made in Boeotia. *c.* 700 B.C. Height 13 ins

26 Clay head from a temple site, Amyclae, near Sparta. Presumably a warrior, wearing a conical helmet. *c.* 700 B.C. Height 4½ ins

on slender tripod legs which are themselves hammered and impressed with Geometric patterns. Later the legs are cast, sometimes with the familiar figure scenes in relief upon them. There are comparatively few small bronze vases. The metal was still somewhat scarce, and was reserved for dedications and, later, the new types of all-bronze armour.

In clay, apart from the simplest figures which show little sophistication, there are oddities like the bell-shaped idols of Boeotia (*Ill. 25*) which were painted up, like vases, and some far more elaborate works in which the features are picked out in paint while the whole heads are careful geometricized studies (*Ill. 26*), far more detailed than the most elaborate of the bronzes.

37

27 Restored clay model of a shrine or house found in a sanctuary at Perachora, but probably made in Argos. It has an apse and a thatched roof was intended. The painted meander need not represent house decoration but is a motif borrowed from pottery for the model. Late eighth century B.C. Height (as restored) 13 ins

Already in the eighth century B.C. Greece offers an assemblage of arts and techniques which begins to recall the variety of Mycenaean art, even if not the riches of Mycenae itself. Only its architecture remains completely unpretentious, with, at the best, one-roomed rectangular or apsidal houses of mud brick with columned porches. Some clay models made in Argos (*Ill. 27*) show these types of house or shrine. Even simpler round huts with central chimneys are reflected in the Cretan model of a 'bathing-hut' shrine complete with removable door, seated goddess, and two Peeping Toms (with their dog) on the roof (*Ill. 28*). There is also a square hut with central

28 Clay model of a 'bathing-hut' shrine from Central Crete. The painted decoration is as on vases of the late ninth century B.C. Height 8⅝ ins

chimney and a bench or sleeping-platform at the back, which has been found in Crete. Several features, however, of the new age represent something more than a natural, local evolution from Proto-geometric art. There is gold jewellery (*Ill. 29*), ivorywork and stone seals, and the non-Greek lions join the Aegean fauna. These are easily assimilated into the Geometric artist's repertory, but they are tokens of a new influence which invited him to exercise his ability in quite other ways. His response and the resultant revolution in the physical appearance of the arts in Greece are the subjects for our next chapter.

29 Ear-ring pendants of gold, with patterns in wire and granulation, and settings for inlays of glass or amber. Eighth century B.C. Diam. 1¼ ins

CHAPTER TWO

Greece and the Arts of the East and Egypt

Greece is a poor country. Its mineral resources are slight and its farmland neither extensive nor very fertile. In the eighth century B.C. the growing population had to look overseas for the materials to satisfy the new appetite, and eventually even for new homes for their families whose own lands had become too small or uncomfortable for them. By about 800 B.C. merchant-adventurers from Euboea and the Greek islands had sailed to the eastern shores of the Mediterranean, along routes already well travelled by the Phoenicians. At the mouth of the River Orontes in North Syria (now part of Turkey) they found the natural outlet for the goods and raw materials from the richer valleys of Mesopotamia, one of the earliest seats of civilization. In a small village (the site is known as Al Mina) they established a trading post beside Cypriots, who were also trading there. As time passed the Cypriot and native elements were swamped by the Greek and the town flourished as a staging post for east–west trade for nearly five hundred years, while in near-by Cilicia, and farther down the coast, other Greeks came in smaller groups to live and trade.

METALWORK

The Greeks brought back with them metals, and consumer goods, including works decorated in styles utterly foreign to the conventions of Greek Geometric art. We find especially bronze bowls decorated in low relief with animals and figure scenes, and ivory plaques carved in low relief as fittings to furniture or toilet articles. Several of these have survived on Greek sites, and there is no doubt much, like textiles or embroidery, which has not. All these things had their effect on both the style of Greek artists' work and the range of their repertory of figures and animals. We can study this most easily in the changes which took place in decorated pottery, but there was a more direct influence too which might be considered first. These were troubled years in the Near East and it seems likely that it was not only goods but craftsmen that were attracted westwards into Greek lands. Certainly there are new techniques of carving and metalwork which appear now for the first time in Greece on objects and in styles which betray the immediate inspiration of foreign craftsmen. Hammered work is prominent—shields with animal-head bosses in Cretan workshops for dedication in the island's shrines and sacred caves, or animal heads projecting like lugs or handles on the deeper cauldrons of Eastern type which are coming to replace the open tripod cauldrons of Geometric Greece. Particularly popular in this position are the griffin heads (*Ill. 30*), and we soon find Greek workshops producing these fine decorative attachments, the later examples being cast and not hammered. The motif is Eastern but the treatment is Greek, and Greek artists soon elaborate the monster's high ears, forehead knob, gaping beak and sinuous neck into an entirely new decorative form. The same happened to the solid cast siren attachments for cauldrons, which are quickly naturalized Greek. In these, as in all other instances of borrowing or inspiration from the East, the Greek artist was discriminate in what he took, and he very soon adapted it according to his own sense of composition or pattern into forms which went far beyond the banal, repetitive designs on the Eastern bronzes or ivories which had prompted them. In this respect the East acted as little more than a catalyst on the development of Greek art, for all the physical changes that it wrought or inspired.

Ivory too was brought from the East. Already in a Geometric grave in Athens we find a group of ivory maidens, naked as the Eastern odalisques or goddesses who inspired them, but slimly built, sharp featured—the Geometric artist's interpretation of an Eastern form. There were various schools of Orientalizing ivory-workshops in Greece. Those in the eastern Greek islands and on the shore of Asia Minor (Ionia), which was an area which the Greeks had settled in the Dark Ages, produced work closer to the Eastern prototypes (*Ill. 31*). This is observed both in the subjects and in the treatment of the human figure—fuller and rounder—a persistent feature of East

30 Three or six bronze griffin heads of this type were fastened below the rims of many Orientalizing bronze cauldrons. The eyes were inlaid, the scales and curls on the neck incised. Late seventh century B.C.

31 An ivory lion from Old Smyrna, of Assyrian type, with folded ear, pointed nose and heavy mane, but probably Greek work. Late seventh century B.C. Length 2¼ ins

Greek art. From East Greece (on Samos) also we have a few examples of small wooden figures carved in a manner very like the ivories. Small carvings travelled far in the Greek world: a clear East Greek type of god and lion was found at Delphi, and on Samos the kneeling youth (*Ill. 32*) may be from mainland Greece, where the forms correspond rather to those of other Greek works in the round, which we have yet to discuss. But it is still difficult to locate the workshops for many of the ivories of this period (*Ill. 33*). In mainland Greece too the Geometric stone seals were being replaced by ivory seals. Some of these took the form of recumbent animals, with the intaglio devices on the base—an Eastern form but a Greek usage. Others—the majority—are disks with simple animal patterns on one or both sides.

Gold was being worked in Greek studios. Artists had learnt from the Easterners or from Egypt the arts of filigree and granulation— the working of gold in wire or tiny globules, the latter a technique which was only rediscovered some thirty years ago. Early gold jewellery in Crete (*Ill. 34*) is close to other Orientalizing work in the island, and in this, as in the other minor arts, we will see mirrored in miniature the figures fashioned on a larger scale in metal or (later) stone.

44

32 (*left*) The kneeling youth in ivory from Samos may be part of the fitting to a lyre. His eyes and pubic hair had been inlaid in other material. The artist has carefully exploited the grain of the ivory. Later seventh century B.C. Height 5¾ ins

33 (*right*) The two girls with their clothes slipping from them may be the daughters of Proitos. They had been sent mad by Hera and ranged over the land of Argos attacking wayfarers. Later seventh century B.C. The ivory group is 5⅜ ins high

34 Gold crescent pendant from near Knossos, with human heads and four birds attached. The eyes of the cable pattern were once filled with amber paste. Early seventh century B.C. Width 2 ins

Work in these new materials and techniques can hardly have been inspired simply by imported articles, and we must suppose that emigrant artists from Syria, Assyria and the metalworking areas of Armenia (then Urartu), had come to Greece in the eighth to seventh century, set up shop, and taught their craft. But the most obvious effects of the Orientalizing wave are observed on painted pottery—a field largely ignored by the Easterner but which, as we have already seen, meant much to the Greeks.

In Eastern figure drawing and carving the Greeks found an art which was as conventional as their own Geometric, but far more realistic. The strictly profile or frontal were the rule but the masses of the body were more accurately observed, and anatomical detail stylized into more realistic patterns. They also found a variety of floral devices such as Geometric art has shunned, both as the principal subject of a pattern and as subsidiary decoration. These new styles had their effect in different ways in the various pottery-producing centres of Greece.

VASE PAINTING

In Corinth, a powerful State guarding the landward approach to the Peloponnese from the north, the Geometric styles of Athens had been copied, as by other Greek States, but the figure scenes were generally avoided and instead we see a fondness for most precise drawing of simple Geometric patterns. This meant that without a strong tradition in figure drawing, like Athens', Corinthian artists were more prepared to accept the new figure styles, and the intricate floral friezes. These they adapted in various ways (*Ill. 35*). The

35 The Protocorinthian painter offers a free version of the Eastern floral pattern on a jug, found at Cumae in Italy. These extravagant essays were short-lived at Corinth. *c.* 700 B.C. Height 13¼ ins

silhouette style of Geometric figure painting was also inadequate when it came to the detailing of eyes, manes and muscles and to showing overlapping figures in vigorous action. The Corinthian painters invented a new technique in which the figures are drawn still in silhouette but details are incised, to show the pale clay beneath in thin clear lines (*Ill. 36*). Red and white paint came to be used also to pick out odd features, like ribs or hair. This new technique we call 'black-figure' and it is practised first on vases called Proto-corinthian by archaeologists (to distinguish them from the later Archaic 'Corinthian' series). At its very best the style is miniaturist (*Ill. 37*), and tiny figures barely one inch high are painted—etched, rather—on the small perfume-flasks (*aryballoi*) which seem to have been one of the most important products of Corinth's potters' quarter. Larger figures are rarely attempted. The decoration is set in friezes around the vase, as it had been in the preceding period. Animals are the main subjects (lions, goats, bulls and birds)—but there are some new monsters too, taken from the East—sphinxes,

36 A Protocorinthian cup, with a dog, showing the incising 'black-figure' technique applied to figures rather larger than the usual at this time in Corinth. Second quarter of the seventh century B.C. Height 7½ ins

37 A Protocorinthian perfume-flask (the 'Macmillan *aryballos*') with its neck and mouth moulded as a lion's head. The painted friezes show florals, a fight, horsemen, a hare-hunt and rays—all on a vase little over 2½ ins high. Mid seventh century B.C.

griffins and similar creatures. These, and the lions, had already appeared on some Geometric vases but then their forms had been geometricized by the artists. Now the new conventions are observed; their bodies fill out, jaws gape, tongues loll, ribs and muscles bulge. The background is now filled with small dot rosettes or abstract motifs just as on the Geometric vases where massed zigzags were used to fill the gaps which the painter dared not leave empty. The creatures generally pace aimlessly around the vase, but sometimes they are posed heraldically facing each other over a floral, itself a version of the Eastern Tree of Life. There are very few scenes with human figures but towards the middle of the seventh century we find more of the heroic episodes as well as a number of battle scenes showing the latest hoplite tactics with disciplined ranks of bronze-clad soldiers (*Ill. 38*). Floral friezes—the Eastern lotus and bud or palmette—appear on the shoulders of the vases, while below the main frieze there may often be a smaller one with a row of animals or a hare-hunt. At the base upward-pointing rays recall the spiky blossoms which decorate the rounded bases of many Eastern and Egyptian vases.

38 A detail from the Protocorinthian 'Chigi vase' in Rome, showing hoplite warriors closing in battle. On the left a piper plays to help the ranks to keep step. There is freer use of colour here (red, browns and white) and on this vase the ordinary animal friezes are suppressed. Mid seventh century B.C., by the same painter as *Ill. 37*. Height of frieze 2 ins

39 Part of a Protoattic clay plaque, dedicated to Athena at Sunium, showing marines on a ship, with a steersman. *c.* 700 B.C.

The Orientalizing vase painting of Athens presents far less of a break and contrast with what went before than does that of Corinth. The new patterns and subjects are admitted, but more slowly. A black-figure technique is not adopted, and instead the details of figures are rendered by line drawing instead of silhouette for heads (*Ill. 39*), and eventually for whole figures. White paint is sometimes used for details (Corinth at this time preferred red) and even a spot of incision here and there. The figures themselves—even of the Eastern monsters and the Greek centaur (*Ill. 40*)—are still rendered very much in the Geometric manner with angular features and bodies. The filling ornament is still largely Geometric and the floral patterns are translated into geometrical constructions rather than simply copied as was usual at Corinth.

40 A Protoattic vase showing a centaur with his prey. The conventions are still very Geometric, but the loops on the body of the vase and the frieze of 'S's are Orientalizing. *c.* 700 B.C. Height 17½ ins

41 The one-eyed giant Polyphemus (Cyclops) is blinded by Odysseus and his companions in his cave, having been reduced to a drunken stupor (notice the cup). From the neck of a Protoattic grave vase, found at Eleusis. Odysseus is differentiated from his companions by the colour of his body. There is some incision (as in black-figure) for the hair, beards and fingers. Mid seventh century B.C. Height of frieze c. 17 ins

At first sight these Athenian vases (called Protoattic) simply look more primitive and outdated beside the Protocorinthian, and they certainly did not travel so far in the Greek world or have the same influence. But they have significant and important redeeming features. First, the monumental character of the Geometric grave-marking vases is not forgotten. On the new vases the figures sometimes stand nearly two feet tall and they present problems of drawing which the miniaturist Protocorinthian painters never had to face. Secondly, the tradition of human figure drawing ensured the continued appearance of narrative (*Ill. 41*) or genre scenes as well as the inevitable incursions of Orientalizing animals and monsters. Thirdly, the technique allowed a far more pictorial treatment and balance of the dark and light masses both in the general composition and the

42 A plate from Thasos, probably made in Naxos. Bellerophon, on the winged horse Pegasus, attacks the Chimaera, which has a lion's body, a goat's head in the small of the back and a serpent tail. Mid seventh century B.C. Diam. 11 ins

43 The griffin jug from Aegina was painted on one of the Cyclades islands. The lion with its prey is an Eastern motif but the grazing horses go back to the Geometric tradition. Notice the floral attachments to the Geometric triangles at the base. Earlier seventh century B.C. Height 15⅜ ins

44 Polyphemus and Odysseus, as in *Ill. 41*, but treated in a rather different manner. The fragment is from Argos, from a vase of Argive shape. The drawing is like Attic work and the washes of paint on the human bodies recall island vases. Mid seventh century B.C.

individual figures. This is enhanced by the mid seventh century by the use of white paint in the so-called 'black-and-white style'. It leads naturally to experiments with broad masses of other colours, or colour washes to cover flesh parts or drapery. This attempt at polychromy is something new on Greek vases. It is also short-lived since it presented technical difficulties. In the seventh and early sixth centuries it was exploited less by Athens than by the Greek islands (*Ill. 42*), where vases of a style and technique broadly analogous to the Athenian were being made. In Crete and occasionally in the islands there was a vogue for vases modelled partly as animals or as human heads. The griffin top to the jug from Aegina (*Ill. 43*) follows a type more familiar to us in bronze. The outline style was practised also in parts of the Peloponnese, despite the proximity of Corinth, as at Argos (*Ill. 44*). It may have been emigrant Argive

55

45 The upper part of an island 'Melian' vase. On the neck women watch a duel over armour. From the body we see part of a lyre-playing Apollo with two Muses in a chariot drawn by winged horses. A brown wash is used on the men's flesh. *c.* 630 B.C. Height of neck 8¾ ins

artists who introduced the style to the Greek colonies in Sicily. On the vases of Melos (?) we can follow the outline, polychrome style until well into the sixth century (*Ill. 45*). The simpler outline drawn styles were affected by the East Greek cities, who were even slower to abandon Geometric patterns and figures. In Rhodes and Ionia a decorative animal frieze style (called the 'wild goat style' after its most popular beast) is adopted in about the middle of the century. It is unpretentious, but in general effect very different from the styles of mainland Greece and has been thought to owe something to Eastern tapestry patterns (*Ill. 46*). It too survives into the sixth century.

OTHER ARTS

The conventions of Greek Orientalizing art, which we best observe in the painted vases, determine also the decoration of other objects and other materials. Besides the painted vases there are large clay

46 A 'wild goat' vase, probably made in Rhodes. On the shoulder is the usual spiral pattern flanked by ducks and griffins; then the friezes of dogs, goats and deer, and the characteristic lotus and bud frieze at the base. Late seventh century B.C.

jars with decoration in low relief. These are best known in Crete, Boeotia and in the Greek islands, and the scenes on them, freely modelled or impressed, introduce us to some new subjects in the artist's repertory, including the Trojan Horse (*Ill. 47*). Engaging small vases in the shape of animals or heads were made as perfume-flasks, and we have already seen the necks of vases moulded as griffins' or lions' heads. Clay and bronze figurines reflect the styles of larger works in stone, and painted clay revetments begin to appear, to protect the wooden parts of buildings, or as decoration on temples and altars (*Ill. 48*). Sheet-bronze is often used for the sheathing of parts of furniture or weapons. On it we find the early technique of hammering with beaten details, for floral or figure

47 The neck of a clay relief vase found in Mykonos in 1961. The Trojan Horse, on wheels. The Greeks within it are shown, as through windows out of which they hold their weapons and armour. Others have 'dismounted' already. Later seventh century B.C.

48 The monstrous Gorgon with her child, the winged horse Pegasus, is the subject of this clay relief which may have decorated the end or side of an altar at Syracuse. Her kneeling posture is the Archaic convention for running or flying. Later seventh century B.C. Height 22 ins

49 Cut-out bronze plaque, decorated in very low relief with incised details, from Crete, and of a type peculiar to Crete. It shows two huntsmen, one with a wild goat (ibex) on his shoulders. Third quarter of the seventh century B.C: Height 7 ins

50 Cut-out bronze plaque from Olympia with incised details showing a mother griffin with her young. This was probably the blazon of a wooden shield. Late seventh century B.C. $31\frac{1}{8} \times 31\frac{1}{2}$ ins

scenes. A different technique involves incision of detail lines and appears at its best on the decorative cut-out plaques made in Crete (*Ill. 49*) and a number of shield blazons found at Olympia. One offers a characteristic Greek treatment of an Eastern monster, tamed and domesticated: a mother griffin suckling her young (*Ill. 50*).

The stone seals which were being cut at the end of the Geometric period were replaced in the Peloponnese by ivory. In the islands, however, an unexpected source inspired an important new school of stone-seal engravers. Fine Mycenaean and Minoan seals found in plundered tombs or in fields were studied by artists on Melos, who copied the shapes of the stones and, as soon as they had mastered the technique, some of the distinctive motifs. For the most part, however, they used the Orientalizing animal and monster devices

51 Impression of an Island Gem. A stag or goat, with dolphins in the field. *c.* 600 B.C. Length 1 in

which we see on island vases (*Ill. 51*). These 'Island Gems'—they were once mistaken for prehistoric stones—provide a continuous tradition of engraving until well into the sixth century, when a new source introduces new shapes and initiates a more fruitful tradition. In the islands again, and East Greece, goldsmiths exploit to the full their newly mastered techniques in some of the finest decorative jewellery we have from antiquity (*Ill. 52*).

SCULPTURE

Of larger works of art in this early period we know very little. Wall paintings there may have been, but we can only guess about them from their hypothetical influence upon vase painting (the

52 A gold roundel. On the petals are pairs of golden flies, human (Dedalic) heads and bulls' heads. Probably made in one of the Greek islands (?Melos) in the second half of the seventh century B.C.

53 Bronze statuette of a man carrying a ram on his shoulders, from Crete. The head is Dedalic, the dress Cretan. Later seventh century B.C. Height 7⅛ ins

influence more likely passed the other way). Wooden sculpture there must have been and there are literary references to early cult statues of wood (*xoana*), but they were probably very primitive in appearance, and nothing wooden has been preserved except for a few statuettes from the waterlogged temple site on Samos. The hammered bronze sheathing of wooden statuettes at Dreros, in Crete, shows forms akin to other early Orientalizing hammered work in bronze and gold.

Soft limestone can be carved almost as easily as wood, and there are stray examples of relief work in an early Orientalizing style, again from Crete. One of the new techniques introduced from the East had been the use of the mould for clay plaques and figures. This means of mass production helped to canonize and stereotype proportions for figures and, especially, the features of a facing head. The type is close to that of the Eastern naked goddess (Astarte) plaques, some of which reached the Greek world and were copied there, although the whole figure of the goddess was soon given clothes and called Aphrodite. But the face is still thoroughly Greek, alert and angular unlike the podgy Easterner. The type—it is called 'Dedalic'—is most commonly met on the mould-made clay figures and plaques, but it is found also on other objects—bronzes (*Ill. 53*), ivories, gold jewellery, stone lamps—and, more important, it is used for limestone statuettes. These are either independent figures (*Ill. 54*), or they appear in the round, standing or seated, as the sculptural embellishment of temple buildings (as later at Prinias, in Crete) which at about this time began to attract such decoration.

This is the fashion after the mid seventh century, but even the largest examples of figures carved in the Dedalic style are little more than decorative statuettes, until a new influence promotes a new scale. The monumental quality which we look for in Greek sculpture needed a more lively source of inspiration than anything the Near East could offer—and it was found in Egypt. Greek mercenaries had been allowed to settle in the Nile Delta after the mid seventh century and a trading town was soon established by the East Greeks and Aeginetans at Naucratis. This brought Greeks and Greek artists into close contact with Egypt for the first time since the Bronze Age. They were impressed by what was least familiar to them—the massive stone statuary and architecture, and it was from this inspiration that the beginnings of Greek monumental sculpture and architecture stem. They had to face the challenge of both size and material, for the Egyptian figures were often of the hardest stones—porphyry and granite. The Greeks looked to the fine white marble which could be so easily quarried on their islands, and which could be worked with iron tools and the emery which these same islands (notably Naxos) could supply. The style of the new figures—of white marble and lifesize or more—is still Dedalic, for these were the only conventions for statuary which the Greek artists could at that time employ in statues of women. We have early examples from Samos and

54 Limestone statuette (the 'Auxerre goddess') of typical Dedalic type, with the usual wig-like hair. The incised lines on the dress outlined the areas of different colours picking out the pattern. The shawl, covering both shoulders, is a Cretan garment. *c.* 630 B.C. Height 24½ ins

55 Marble *kouros* (part of the face, including the nose, the left arm and leg restored) dedicated to Poseidon at Sunium in Attica. The marble is from one of the Greek islands. *c.* 600 B.C. Height *c.* 10 ft

Delos (the dedication of Nikandre). The males too at first follow the Dedalic conventions for the head, but the body is shown naked (but for a belt), long-limbed, one foot set just before the other in a pose which lent stability, and had been used before in bronze statuettes. It owes nothing to the stiff Egyptian figures which appear rooted to the ground. The earliest of these statues of youths—*kouroi*—are from the islands and there is a distinguished group from Attica from about 600 B.C. (*Ill. 55*). At this early date the anatomical detail is translated into pure pattern—ears, knee-caps, ribs—not related organically to the body, which is itself foursquare, perceptibly imprisoned still in the rectangular block on which its outlines had been drawn and from which it had been painstakingly chipped.

Monumental stone architecture in Greece owned the same source of inspiration as the sculpture—Egypt. The effect was felt at about the same time, but the development was slower and is best discussed in the next chapter. It must be mentioned here because these two phenomena mark an important stage in the progress of Greek art: the establishment of new crafts in which the Greek artist was to find his most fully satisfying media of expression.

The motley of seventh-century Greek art is as confusing as it is brilliant. Local schools flourish and propagate individual new styles. New techniques are learnt, and often improved upon. The Greek artist took note of the exotic and grandiose works of those older civilizations with which his world had now regained contact. He borrowed and adapted as he thought fit, imposing his native sense of pattern and standards of precision on the stereotyped forms of the foreigners' arts. Because of the paramount importance of Greek art in later centuries we tend sometimes to assume that it had always been so independent, and always the teacher rather than the taught. It is well to remember how little this is true of some of the most important formative years. It is equally important to remember the strength of the tradition which had its beginnings far earlier than the arrival of new ideas from overseas, and was able to translate these new ideas into forms in which we recognize the origins of Classical art.

CHAPTER THREE

Archaic Greek Art

The sixth century sees the consolidation of the prosperity of the States of mainland Greece with the rule of benevolent tyrants (or at least not 'tyrannical' in our sense of the word) giving place already in some cities to democratic constitutions. The city-states remain independent of each other, and often at war, but there was a growing sense of nationality, of the difference between the Greeks and the rest—the barbarians. The new prosperity went hand-in-hand with vigorous trading around the shores of the Mediterranean, and the rapid growth of the colonies—in Sicily, Italy and on the shores of the Black Sea—which had been founded in past generations to ease problems of land at home. One result of all this was that the Greeks made some enemies overseas as a nation (although there were always a few fellow-travellers) and not simply as individual States. In the west there were the Carthaginians and the Etruscans, their

56 The Temple of Apollo at Corinth; the earliest Doric temple in Greece with some of its columns still standing. Mid sixth century B.C.

57 The Doric Temple of Hera (the so-called 'Basilica') at Paestum. A good example of the early cigar-shaped columns with bulging capitals. Mid sixth century B.C.

rivals and customers in trade, and in the east the new empire of Persia. In the early fifth century they had to face these enemies with force of arms. They survived the encounters and made sure that for a while at least their troubles would be with their fellows rather than with foreigners. In the century or more leading up to this the arts of the Greek world and its different schools also moved closer to a common style, usually under the influence of the dominant cities in each craft—Athens for pottery, the Peloponnesian cities for bronze-work. Regional differences are still readily perceptible, however, and one of the features of sixth-century art is the contribution made by East Greek artists working away from home, many no doubt as refugees from the Persians.

The new arts of monumental architecture and sculpture present the most striking monuments of this, as of succeeding centuries; indeed the sheer size of some building projects in the East Greek cities remained unrivalled until after the Classical period.

ARCHITECTURE

The architectural achievements of the Egyptians had had a rather different effect on the Greeks from that of their sculpture. Hitherto the Greeks had been used to fairly simple brick or stone structures with no decorative elaboration beyond the occasional use of a sculptural frieze on walls, in the Eastern manner. In Egypt they saw massive stone architecture and stone columns with carved capitals and bases. These were virtually unknown in the Near East, but in Greece already at least one temple (on Samos) had been given an encircling colonnade in the seventh century and the Greeks were not slow to take the hint about the elaboration of this feature which was to prove such an integral element in their architecture.

The beginnings of the major stone orders of architecture in Greece can be traced back to the end of the seventh century. In mainland Greece the Doric order was evolved, with simple columns, reminiscent of both Mycenaean and Egyptian types, having cushion capitals, fluted shafts and no bases (*Ill. 56*). The upper works were divided rhythmically into a frieze of triglyphs (the vertical bands) and metopes (often sculptured) which were a free adaptation of the woodwork in these parts of earlier buildings. This was the style popular in the western Greek colonies also (*Ill. 57*). In East Greece and the islands the other major order of stone architecture, the Ionic, borrowed its decorative forms from the repertory of Orientalizing art, with volutes and florals which in the Near East had never graced anything larger than wooden or bronze furniture, or—like the volute capitals of Phoenicia—had never formed an element of any true architectural order. The first capitals (known at Smyrna and Phocaea) are bell-shaped with floral patterns in relief upon them. They are followed by the Aeolic capitals, with the volutes springing from the shafts, which give way to the broader Ionic, with the volutes eventually linked. The shafts have more flutes than the Doric,

58 The Naxian sphinx at Delphi. Columns often support dedications in the Archaic period. This shows one of the earliest Ionic capitals, with wide-set concave volutes, which were probably separated in the centre by a floral (now missing). *c.* 560 B.C. Height of sphinx 92 ins

59 A restoration (by F. Krischen) of the side front of the Temple of Artemis at Ephesus. Designed in the 540s, completed a century later

with, in time, flat ridges between them. There are bases too—swelling *tori* and disks, elaborately fluted like carefully turned wooden furniture. Some of the earliest Ionic columns served as bases for votive statues, like the sphinx dedications made by Naxians at Delphi (*Ill. 58*) and on Delos. On Ionic buildings the upper works over the colonnades are simpler than the Doric, but an important feature is the running frieze, which is sometimes carved. Altogether there is much more variety in the Ionic order, with much more superficial ornament and decoration (*Ill. 59*). It seems ornate and fussy beside the Doric, and the contrast was one happily exploited by architects of the Classical period, as we shall see.

The orders were applied to the exteriors of temples, which retained their simple plan, of porch and hall (*cella*) where the cult statue stood,

71

60 Carved lotus and palmette frieze from the Siphnian Treasury at Delphi. This ran beneath the overhanging gutter. *c.* 525 B.C. Later florals have slimmer, more flaring leaves

but were now regularly surrounded by a colonnade. Smaller structures, the pavilions or treasuries set up by individual States at the national sanctuaries, have columns at the front only and on Ionic treasuries at Delphi we find statues of girls, caryatides, replacing the columns in the porch. The largest buildings, on the other hand, might double the rows of columns at the sides and even treble those at the front (as at Samos and Ephesus). Inside the *cella* more columns helped to support the roof and provided a nave-like approach to the cult statue. Altars stood outside the front door of the temple, in the east, and were either simple rectangular blocks with carved upper parts, or, in East Greece, monumental structures with broad flights of steps leading up to the sacrificial platform. Where wood was still used on the exterior of temples it was protected by painted clay revetments, but generally walls are all stone now, of precisely jointed rectangular ashlars, or, for some house and terrace walls, of polygonal blocks, sometimes with curved edges (the so-called Lesbian) which are no less precisely fitted. Ionic buildings especially were decorated with elaborately carved mouldings (*Ill. 60*), around doors, along the tops of walls, on gutters and over the columns, sometimes even on the columns. Similar floral and volute mouldings are repeated in many minor works of bronze or clay, and in painting, and they are successors to the Orientalizing florals and subsidiary ornaments. The sculptural decoration of temples will be discussed later in this chapter.

We have of necessity so far spoken only of temples. It was for these houses of the gods that the elaboration of the stone orders was reserved at first, and not for private houses, which probably boasted little more than painted wooden exteriors. The colonnade shelters (*stoai*) and entrance gates to sanctuaries were also treated in the grand manner, but only in the succeeding period do public buildings, law courts and theatres, regularly attract this attention.

SCULPTURE

Of the statuary in the round the *kouros* figures of naked youths, with their set, symmetrical stance, hands clenched at the sides, one foot advanced, remain unchanged in pose throughout our period, and so serve as a useful standard on which to observe the advances in technique and treatment which appear in different ways on other figures.

The *kouroi* were long known as Apollos, but few can represent that or any other deity; most are dedicated as attendants to a god, while others stand as memorials—not portraits—over graves. Through the sixth century we can observe that a growing confidence in the carving of marble, and the use of chisels where at first all the work was done with punches and abrasives, lead to the disappearance of the block-like character of the earliest in the series (as *Ill. 55*). Anatomical details become more realistically treated and are better related to the mass and structure of the body (*Ill. 61*). The Archaic smile, which came into fashion in the second quarter of the century, is relaxed into a straighter, sometimes sulky expression. The convention had given an impression of strained cheerfulness which the

61 Marble *kouros*, lifesize, from a cemetery in the countryside of Attica (Anavysos). On the base was inscribed the verse—'Stop and grieve at the tomb of the dead Kroisos, slain by wild Ares in the front rank of battle.' *c.* 540 B.C.

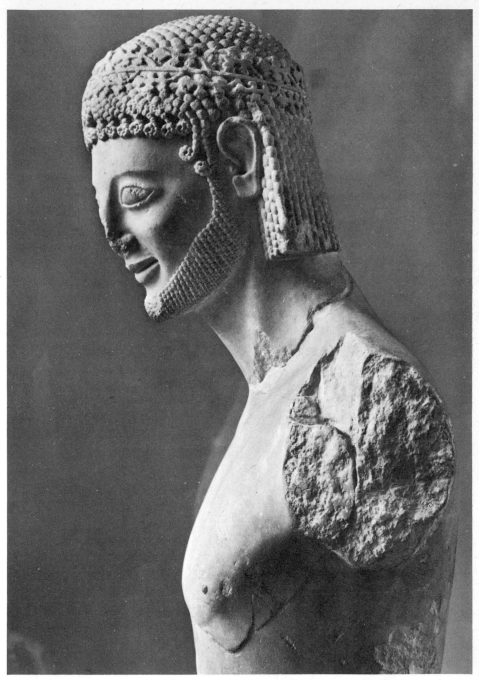

62 The 'Rampin horseman', a dedication on the Acropolis at Athens. The head was removed from Athens before the excavations which yielded the body and is still in the Louvre. Mid sixth century B.C.

artist may have appreciated, but which was usually quite alien to what we expect of Greek funerary or votive art, and which cannot fairly be added to the few instances of emotion expressed in the features of Archaic statues. The figures are seldom now colossi, more than lifesize, and this, together with the improved techniques, contributes to the impressive advance in realism which is achieved within the rigid convention of the pose. The body and its parts are still treated as pattern compositions by the artist, and this approach, which persists into the Classical period, is in no way impaired by the closer approximation to nature.

There are other free-standing statues of men which do not observe the *kouros* pose: from the Acropolis at Athens comes the famous calf-bearer and a series of horsemen. One of these is the 'Rampin horseman' (*Ill. 62*). In the head we observe the Archaic smile; the exquisitely precise carving of the marble in curving planes meeting in sharp ridges which would have been picked out even more dramatically in brilliant sunshine; and the meticulous and heavy treatment of the curls and locks of this young Athenian cavalier dandy, whose oak wreath tells of his success in the games. Here too the strict frontality of the *kouroi* is relaxed. The head is inclined down and to one side, towards the spectator who would be passing across the front of the horse.

We have seen the way in which the artist treated the male body almost as an exercise in pattern and composition. In a country and society in which the fair sex was not seen in public as much undressed as it is today, it is not wholly surprising that female figure studies were not common in statuary until command of technique allowed a successful suggestion of the more sensuous qualities. In vase painting it is otherwise, as we shall see. To the Archaic sculptor, however, women were little more than clothes-hangers. Faces are rarely any prettier or more appealing than those of the men, the hair not always more ornate. Patterns of folds, heavy and straight, fanning out across the body, or gathering into a zigzag hemline, exercised the sculptor's imagination and taste for variety of pattern. Breasts are admitted to exist, but not much admired. On later *korai* (maidens) the material is drawn tightly around the legs to show them

63 The 'Berlin goddess', from the countryside of Attica (Keratea). She is holding a pomegranate and wearing a *polos* head-dress. Early sixth century B.C. Height 77 ins

and the buttocks as though bare, but the gesture and motif was one designed at first simply to offer a pattern of diagonal folds across the lower half of the figure. One early *kore* from Attica (*Ill. 63*) is, as a statue of a woman, gaunt and clumsy, redeemed only by the bold carving and simple drapery. The outer garment is the heavy *peplos*.

64 The 'peplos kore' from the Athenian Acropolis. A bronze wreath and ear-rings had been added separately. Her hair and lips are painted red; lashes and brows black; and the patterns on her dress green. *c.* 530 B.C. Height 48 ins

65 A *kore* from the Athenian Acropolis, certainly the work of an Ionian artist, probably a Chian. She wears a *chiton* and *himation*. The *chiton* was blue, and red and blue were used in the patterns on her dress, ear-rings and necklet. *c.* 525 B.C. Preserved height 22 ins

This is the dress of what is perhaps the finest of the ladies from Athens, the '*peplos kore*' (*Ill. 64*), but it was not a garment which fully satisfied the Archaic artist's love of pattern. A new fashion and a new sculptural treatment of drapery arrived together from overseas. At this time in East Greece sculptors were experimenting with ways of diversifying the surface of the carved drapery, suggesting the folds by incised wavy lines or close-set, shallowly carved grooves. The lighter and more voluminous *chiton*, which Athenian *korai* had worn as an undershift, lent itself more to this sort of treatment, offering full sleeves and skirts which could be gathered into a multiplicity of folds. These were further varied by drawing aside the skirt, in the manner which was later to show off the legs, by slinging the *himation* or cloak diagonally across the upper body to answer the folds across the legs, and by painting the elaborate patterns of embroidered hems. These new '*chiton korai*' (*Ill. 66*) have their effect on the series known to us from the finds on the Athenian Acropolis from about the mid sixth century on, and there is evidence from signed bases and the style of some pieces that East Greek artists (like Archermos of Chios) were in fact at work in the city (*Ill. 65*). Under the influence of these men (mainly Ionians and islanders) some of the *kore* heads even begin to look feminine. Towards the end of the Archaic period more attention is paid to the form of the body beneath the drapery and the features change as did those of the *kouroi*.

All these statues in the round are very much 'set-pieces', offering no variety of pose. For more ambitious sculptural compositions we have to look for work in relief, especially on buildings. The arts of sculpture and architecture in Greece were inspired by the same source and always went hand-in-hand. The architecture was never simply the vehicle for the sculptor, nor was the sculpture merely decoration: its position enhanced and helped to articulate parts of the building and its themes added something to the sanctity of the temple. On Doric buildings the sculptor filled the rectangular metopes with individual groups of two or more figures. Fights are a natural choice but pursuits are found too, and occasionally the action is carried across from one metope to the next. Series of metopes may be linked by a theme—like the Argonauts' story on the Sicyonian building at

66 A *kore* from the Athenian Acropolis wearing a *chiton* only, pulling her skirt tight in front of her. *c.* 510 B.C.

Delphi, or the deeds of Theseus and Heracles on the Athenian Treasury at the same sanctuary. Some of the early metope compositions are the most bold, with frontal views of horsemen, the proud march of the heroes turned cattle rustlers (*Ill. 67*), and the duels of men, or man and monster.

The low triangles at the ends of gabled roofs—pediments—offered an awkward field. At first it is filled by a massive central figure, flanked by other figures or groups at different scales, out towards the corners which were conveniently filled by prostrate bodies. Sometimes a single theme or story occupies the composition, but the diminishing scale away from the centre does not make for unity, and in some instances looks rather ridiculous. Fish or snake-

67 A metope from a Sicyonian building at Delphi. Castor and Polydeuces, Idas and Lynceus, stole cattle in the course of the Argonaut expedition. Heroes and cattle march in step, the beasts held in by the spears. Names were painted on the background. *c.* 560 B.C.

68 A limestone group in the corner of a pediment from a building on the Athenian Acropolis. These may be personifications of winds, holding attributes, their winged serpent bodies entwined. Hair and beards are blue, eyes black, skin yellow; and there is black and red on the feathers and scaly stripes. *c.* 560 B.C. Height of foremost bearded figure 28 ins

tailed monsters were favourites for corners, like the entwined wind demons with snake tails from Athena's Temple on the Acropolis at Athens (*Ill. 68*). These, like many such early architectural sculptures, are carved in limestone, which is, if necessary, covered with a coat of stucco to provide a smooth surface, and is brilliantly painted. The backgrounds were painted deep blue or red to help the lighter figures stand out from the shadows of the gables. By the end of the Archaic period unity of scale is observed for all the figures in the pediment, except the central divinity, and battle scenes were found (at Aegina and Athens) to provide the sort of stooping, falling or recumbent figures to fill the awkward frames (*Ill. 69*).

The sculptures on Ionic buildings are applied according to less rigid rules—or rather, individual and local tastes were given free expression. Of the massive Temple of Artemis at Ephesus we have

83

only scraps of relief figures which decorated the lowest drums of the columns and friezes from the gutter and, perhaps, the *cella* wall. A better example of Ionic architectural sculpture is afforded by the Treasury dedicated by the islanders of Siphnos at Delphi in about 525 B.C. Here the porch columns are replaced by *korai*—caryatides; there are rich floral carvings (as *Ill. 60*) around the door and at the gutter, and figure friezes run on all sides just below the roof. They offer very different answers to the problem of composing a narrative frieze; and the hands of two artists of strongly differing temperament can be detected (east and north by one; west and south by the other). On the north there is the battle of gods and giants (*Ill. 70*), surging across the frieze in such a way as to obscure the divisions between individual duels and encounters; on the west there is the tripartite treatment of the Judgment of Paris, each goddess with her chariot, in which the story is conveyed by telling details of gesture; on the east a Trojan episode, where on one half we see the gods sitting in

69 A warrior from the pediment of the Temple of Aphaea, Aegina. The statues from Aegina were much restored and worked over by the sculptor Thorwaldsen before exhibition in Munich. *c.* 500 B.C.

70 From the north frieze of the Siphnian Treasury at Delphi. Apollo and Artemis stride forward together, drawing their bows (missing); beyond them a giant is fleeing. *c.* 525 B.C.

council on Olympus, on the other a duel of heroes on the Trojan plain; and on the south a most fragmentary processional version of the Rape of the Daughters of Leucippus by the Dioscuri.

Finally there are the acroteria which appear on both Doric and Ionic buildings—figures in the round at gable corners and crown, generally of monsters, sphinxes, griffins, or gorgons.

The sculpture on these buildings, especially in the later pediments, is almost in the round, but the poses and groups shown are far more ambitious than any for free-standing statuary in this period. We have rather to compare the figure drawing on vases, and in fact all Archaic relief sculpture is readily explained in terms of the line drawing on the uncut block, from which the sculpture started. Where the relief was shallow it meant that all the detail was brought to the front plane, even though the figures were shown as overlapping. Only on the very high relief of some metopes and pediments, where the figures are mainly or wholly detached from the background, do we

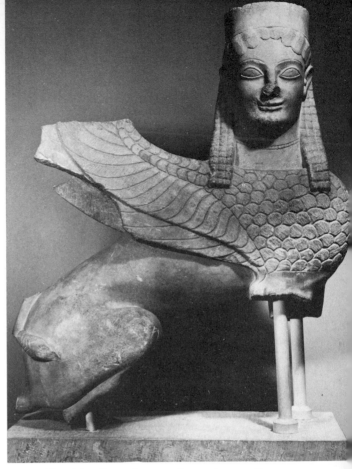

71 Marble sphinx from the top of a gravestone. From a cemetery in the countryside of Attica (at Spata). She wears a *polos* (compare *Ill. 63*). *c.* 570 B.C. Height 18 ins

72 Gravestone of Aristion, signed by the artist Aristocles. The background was painted red. There are traces of red and blue on the figure and the patterns on the corselet show up where the surface has weathered differently. *c.* 510 B.C. Height without base 96 ins

have works carved properly in the round, allowing intelligible three-quarter views. But the compositions remain the same, uninhibited by the greater difficulties presented by the carving.

Shallow relief, picked out in colour, was used for another class of monuments—gravestones. We know best those of Athens. At the start of the sixth century the gravestones were tall shafts (*stelai*) topped by sphinxes (*Ill. 71*), but soon the shaft was carved in relief with a representation of the dead. Youths are shown as athletes, shouldering a discus or holding their oil-bottles, men as warriors (*Ill. 72*): all in an upright stance, like profile views of the *kouroi* they so much resemble in the detail of their carving. A youth is once shown with his young sister, another fragmentary stone has a mother holding her dead child, but it is rare that the tall thin shafts carry more than one figure. These reliefs represent the dead without being real portraits (*kouroi* too could serve as grave-markers, as did also some *korai* in East Greece). The distinctions between adolescence, youth, and middle-age are broadly observed and what might be called generalized portraiture is seen in the puffy features of a boxer.

After about 530 the sphinxes on gravestones were replaced by simpler palmette finials. This is another example of East Greek influence in Athens, for the type had been known in Ionia for a generation already, although the shafts there were not normally carved. The type with the slim tall shaft was abandoned in Athens before the Persian Wars, but persisted in the islands (see *Ill. 115*).

73 Relief from a statue base, which had been built into Athens' walls just after the Persian Wars. It shows athletes training: a runner in the usual starting position with one foot only a little advanced; wrestlers grappling; and a youth testing the point of his javelin. Late sixth century B.C. Length 32 ins

74 Marble votive relief from the Athenian Acropolis showing a figure mounting a chariot. End of the sixth century B.C.

Reliefs appear on other monuments as well. Statue and *stele* bases may be so decorated. Several of these have been found in Athens' main cemetery, carved with scenes of athletes (*Ill. 73*) or young men taking their ease. They also served as votive offerings in sanctuaries. These votive reliefs (*Ill. 74*) may be carved with representations of the deity, or of an act of worship in which the dedicator may be thought to figure among the worshippers. Some show the dedicator alone, like the potter reliefs from the Athenian Acropolis. The best of these reliefs were set in the rock or stood upon pillars. Indeed, apart from the temple itself, the greater part of the decoration of a Greek sanctuary was made up of private dedications set in positions of honour or obscurity according to their size or merit, or to the relative importance and popularity of the dedicator. These personal or State commissions to architects and sculptors are an important feature of Archaic Greece. The artist is hired to do a job, to please or impress mortals or divinities. 'Art for art's sake' was an unnecessary conception.

With these monumental arts already so well established in Greece in the Archaic period it is inevitable that they take pride of place over what is still our most bountiful source of information about Greek art and taste—vase painting.

VASE PAINTING

By the end of the seventh century the Athenian vase painter had adopted wholeheartedly the black-figure technique, which had already been practised at Corinth for a century. With it came also the animal frieze style of Corinth, and for a generation or more the greater part of Athens' vases is covered with rows of animals— lions, goats, boars, sphinxes. But the monumental character of Athens' pottery had not been forgotten, and while at Corinth the gross creatures wandered lost in a maze of filling rosettes in a repetitive, mass-produced style, the Athenian beasts were better managed. The Nessos Painter (a scholarly sobriquet, such as is necessary for anonymous Greek vase painters), was one of the first to use black-figure in Athens (*Ill. 75*). He still painted large funeral vases, and beasts upon them are commensurately massive, precisely

75 Detail of a grave vase, from a cemetery at Vari, in the countryside of Attica. Notice the way the horse's head is pushed to the foreground of the picture. This is an early example of full black-figure in Athens. By the Nessos Painter. *c.* 620 B.C.

ESEN
EN

and boldly drawn in a manner not matched in Corinth. And the narrative scenes persist beside the animals on many vases, generally taking the prior position. The success of this new style in Athenian black-figure pottery is shown by the way it rapidly penetrates markets hitherto served only by Corinthian wares.

The Nessos Painter was succeeded, early in the sixth century, by others who worked in the animal frieze style as well as with narrative scenes, but by about 570 Athenian interest in figure scenes rather than animals is beginning to win the day. The 'François vase', a wine-mixing-bowl (*crater*) found in an Etruscan grave (the Etruscans were always good customers for Greek vases) carries six figured friezes on either side, of which only one is occupied by animals—fighting and posed heraldically over florals, while on the rest and on the handles more than two hundred figures act out mythological scenes (*Ill. 76*). Almost all the figures, and some objects, are labelled with their names and both potter and painter, Ergotimos and Kleitias, signed their work. From now on animal friezes and florals are suppressed to subsidiary positions and the painter increases his repertory of

76 Detail of the 'François vase', painted in Athens by Kleitias. It shows the ship coming to pick up Theseus with the young Athenians he rescued from the Minotaur. One eager sailor swims for shore, while to the right the dance of victory (the *geranos* or crane dance) begins. *c.* 570 B.C. Height of frieze 2½ ins

77 Athenian plate, with a gorgoneion. Even on black-figure vases these heads are drawn in the older outline techniques. Painted by Lydos, *c*. 560 B.C. Diam. 9½ ins

mythological themes. Even the gorgoneion which serves to fill many circular fields in cups or on plates (*Ill. 77*) in the sixth century, is the product of an adventure, also shown on vases—Perseus's encounter with the Gorgon, Medusa and his removal of her (literally) petrifying head. The same head appears often as a device on shields (back to Agamemnon's shield in Homer).

New artists set high standards in painting table vases (the big funeral vases had gone out of fashion). The Amasis Painter's lithe figures show an unexpected, vivid humour. His potter-work is equally individual and it is likely that we have here to deal with a painter-potter of rare distinction (*Ill. 78*). His contemporary (of the mid-century and after) Exekias offers a strong contrast in an almost Classical style with figures of dignity and presence (*Ill. 79*). The vases these artists decorate are wine- or olive-oil-jars (*amphorae*), water-jars (*hydriae*) or wine-mixing-bowls (*craters*). On cups we find a more miniaturist style reminiscent of Protocorinthian. Greek cups generally have two horizontal side handles. The Corinthian type, with a deep bowl, was replaced in Athens by varieties with a broad shallow bowl set on a high splaying stem, like that of a wine-glass. These may have their lips plain (lip cups) with small figures or groups decorating them, or black (band cups) with figures in the band between the handles (*Ill. 80*). Inside there may be a figure or group within a circle, and the rest of the vase is painted with the fine, lustrous black paint which is one of the most appealing features of all good Athenian vases.

78 Athenian black-figure *amphora* by the Amasis Painter. Dionysus, with dancing youths and girls. Notice the way the girls' flesh is drawn in outline and not painted white, as is usual in black-figure. *c.* 540 B.C.

79 Detail from an Athenian black-figure *amphora* by Exekias showing Achilles slaying the Amazon queen Penthesilea at Troy. *c.* 540 B.C.

80 Athenian black-figure band cup. Detail showing lions and a leopard attacking a bull and a mule. *c.* 540 B.C.

81 Corinthian *crater* showing a married couple in a chariot, with friends. Red and white are freely used and the detail on the white parts is painted, not incised. The background is artificially reddened to imitate Athenian vases. Painted by the Three Maidens Painter, *c.* 560 B.C. Height 16¾ ins

   The painters of the later part of the sixth century offer a somewhat racier, sometimes sketchy, style. It occasionally succeeds in combining the precision of Exekias with the new verve, but the influence is now that of another vase-painting technique, 'red-figure', to which we must turn in a moment. Before we do, it should be admitted that not all the fine black-figure vases of the sixth century are Athenian. The Corinthians continued in brisk competition (*Ill. 82*) for the first half of the century, imitating the figure scenes of Athenian vases, even copying the distinctive red colour of·their clay and hiding the finer buff surface of their usual ware (*Ill. 81*). But the output of painted

82 Corinthian black-figure plate showing two sphinxes, with male, bearded heads and floral crowns, posed heraldically on another floral. Notice the lavish use of red paint on bodies, wings and faces. Early sixth century B.C. Diam. 11 ins

pottery for export seems to have been an important factor in Corinth's potters' quarter, especially the colourful *craters* which were sent west to Etruria. When the markets were successfully won by Athenian wares the painters went out of business and the long and distinguished series of figure-decorated Corinthian vases came to an end.

Other schools, dependent in varying degrees upon Corinth and Athens, produced black-figure vases for their local markets. Spartan cups had some success overseas but their figures are stiff and lifeless though often very precisely drawn (*Ill. 83*). Such East Greek schools as were not ringing the changes on the old outline style of the wild

83 Spartan black-figure cup, the name-piece of the Hunt Painter, who specializes in these unusual 'porthole' views with the figures cut off by the circle frame. A boar hunt is in progress; the beast has a broken throwing-spear in its back. *c.* 550 B.C. Diam. 7⅝ ins

goats, also produced black-figure, generally fussy and highly coloured, but also some delicate cups of great charm and originality (*Ill. 84*). On these, and the Spartan cups, we often see whirling compositions, or scenes which own no top or bottom, such as the Athenian artists generally eschewed; and more of the interior is filled with the scene. In the west Chalcidian potters had set up shop perhaps in Rhegium (Reggio) and had some success in Italy and Sicily with vases on which the finer motifs of the other schools were combined with a superb decorative sensibility and telling economy of line (*Ill. 85*). Emigrant artists from East Greece had some success in Etruria and promoted distinguished local schools of black-figure. An Ionian artist working

84 East Greek cup, perhaps made on Samos. The detail is not in fact incised but left in reserved lines. A man dances between two trees. To the left a bird is bringing food to fledgelings in the nest, and there is a cicada on a branch. *c.* 550 B.C. Diam. 9 ins

in Caere (Cervetri) made a series of superbly colourful *hydriae* which were in some demand locally (*Ill. 86*). He shows a rare sense of humour as well as imagination in his treatment of myth—sometimes the story is outside the usual vase painters' repertory.

Although the individuality of these schools, and of the different artists in Athens, can be appreciated at a glance, there were fairly rigidly observed conventions in black-figure, and an overall unity of style which developed slowly. The black silhouette with incised detail remained the basic element. Red was used more often than in the seventh century—for hair and beards, on drapery, and for a while in early black-figure to show masculine sunburnt faces. Women's faces and bodies are in white, painted over the black silhouette which showed through the incised details, and white appears on drapery patterns. The male-red, female-white convention was observed in Egyptian art, and is, after all, an approximation to life. The figures are shown in a strictly profile view although it was usually found easier to show the chest frontal, especially in moving figures. For running or flying the figures appear as kneeling with elbows thrown high. The eye too is frontal even in a profile head, a disk for men, almond shape for women, on Athens' vases. Frontal heads and bodies are rare except for grotesque or horrific creatures like satyrs, centaurs and gorgons. The representation of drapery changes from flat enveloping folds to elaborately patterned pleats

85 Chalcidian black-figure column *crater* (a mixing-bowl) with cocks and snakes. Note the characteristically plump buds in the floral. *c.* 530 B.C. Height 14½ ins

86 A Caeretan *hydria*, one of the most colourful classes of Greek black-figure vases. Heracles is delivering the hound of Hades, Cerberus, to his master Eurystheus, who has jumped, terrified, into a storage jar. *c.* 530 B.C. Height 16⅝ ins

and zigzag hems, exactly like the carving of the *korai* after the mid-century. Emotion is expressed by gesture—hands tearing hair in grief, gestures of farewell, of animated conversation, of abandoned joy; rarely a facial detail like a furrowed brow or clenched teeth. The women are ageless, with an occasional matron. For the men a beard marks maturity or status, and white hair or partial baldness and bent shoulders old age.

Conventions, too, govern the way in which the more popular scenes are shown, and the accepted way of depicting, for instance, the Judgment of Paris is rarely changed or abandoned by artists. But within these conventions individual skill and imagination could still be expressed. Scenes of myth predominate, especially the deeds of popular heroes like Heracles (*Ill. 87*). There are also more formal studies of the gods, alone or in groups. Many of the vases are designed to serve a drinking-party, and scenes with the god of wine, Dionysus, are naturally common. In his entourage is one of the most engaging figures of Archaic art—the satyr. An earlier poet had called satyrs 'unemployable layabouts'. Not until the sixth century did artists

87 Detail from an Athenian black-figure *amphora*, painted by Psiax. Heracles has to wrestle with the Nemean lion since it cannot be hurt by ordinary weapons. The incision on later black-figure vases is often much lighter, recalling the brushwork of red-figure. *c.* 520 B.C.

look for a way of showing these uninhibited creatures and their embarrassingly human weaknesses. The centaur type, part man, part horse, may have suggested the physical form, since the satyr (see *Ills. 93, 94, 96*) is little more than an abbreviated centaur, with shaggy head, horse's ears and tail, and two human or horse's legs (a combination of the two in East Greek art). The centaurs had shown a fondness for wine and women; the satyrs added song, and in Dionysus's service they even play a part in the early development of the Greek theatre.

Besides these scenes of myth everyday life was not neglected— weddings, burials, gossip at the fountain, courtship and love, and, of course, the drinking-party; but some of the finest examples of these subjects, and an even greater range of them, are to be found on Athenian vases of the new technique, which succeeded black-figure.

The black-figure vases were still being made in the fifth century, but in their last phase they take second place—except for some traditional prize vases which perpetuate the old technique (the Panathenaic *amphorae*)—to vases painted in what we call the 'red-figure' style. This had been invented in Athens about 530 B.C. It is an exact reversal of black-figure. The background now, and not the figure, is painted black, and so the figures appear in the red colour of the clay ground, and the details are painted upon them in line detail where before they had been incised (*Ill. 88*). In fact we are back with the outline drawings of the Orientalizing period, which had never been quite forgotten, even by some black-figure artists (like Sophilos and the Amasis Painter). The brush is a more subtle implement than the incising point, and although at first treatment of figures and detail is not much different from black-figure, in time the more flowing line assists the more realistic rendering of anatomy and drapery. The fact that the outline of the figure is limited by a line, and not the outer edge of the silhouette mass, also has its effect. Colour now plays virtually no part, and only the lightest touches of red and white—even occasionally gilding—appear, but variety is admitted by the use of thinned paint for light anatomical detail, fine drapery or hair, and a relief line of brilliance and body for more important outlines and strokes. Men and women have to be

88 Detail from an Athenian red-figure vase by the Andocides Painter, showing the goddess Artemis wearing *chiton*, shawl, wreath and elaborate ear-rings. Incision is still used around her hair. She holds flowers, stylized into scrolls, while she unconcernedly witnesses a contest between her brother Heracles and Apollo. *c.* 525 B.C.

89 Centrepiece of an Athenian red-figure cup. A naked girl kneels before an altar holding a wreath. The flames on the altar and the wreath are painted red. Late sixth century B.C.

distinguished by features, dress and anatomy now, not colour. The line of the body is sketched through the intricate drapery patterns and there are plenty of brilliant and perceptive studies of the female nude (*Ill. 89*) which we look for in vain in sculpture of this date. The musculature of the male body is more accurately observed, the abrupt transition between frontal chest and profile hips is managed plausibly, and even back three-quarter views and bold foreshortening of limbs are brought off. The eye is gradually shown in a proper profile view, but frontal heads are still avoided, and three-quarter views of heads not attempted. There are even a few examples of light shading which helps to lend an illusion of mass to the linear drawing.

The earliest of the red-figure artists, the Andocides Painter (*Ill. 88*) decorated vases which also carried scenes in the old black-figure technique (done by him or a companion) and other artists produced these bilinguals. The new style had its effect on the old—quite apart from the way in which it gradually stifled it. Subjects and stories remain unchanged but we see rather more specialization among the painters, who are attracted to work on either large or small vases (usually cups). The first half-century of red-figure produced most of its great masters. Artists like Euphronios and Euthymides (*Ill. 90*) were working before 500 in what might be termed the Classic style which owed something to the work of Exekias and for its precision

90 (*left*) Red-figure *amphora* painted by Euthymides showing elderly revellers. The inscription (invisible here) on the left is a friendly challenge to a contemporary artist—'as never Euphronios'. The figures offer early and successful studies of difficult three-quarter views. *c.* 510 B.C. Height 23⅝ ins

91 (*right*) Red-figure vase by Oltos, with a girl tying on her sandals and a satyr struggling with a nymph. This shape of *amphora* copies an Etruscan type and was adopted by Athenian potters with an eye to the Etruscan market. *c.* 520 B.C. Height 15⅛ ins

92 Clay plaque from the Athenian Acropolis, probably painted by Euthymides. It bore the inscribed motto 'Megacles is handsome', but the name was erased and that of Glaukytes substituted, probably after Megacles had been ostracized in 486 B.C. *c.* 500 B.C. Width 20 ins

and command of line can compare with the very best in contemporary statuary. Euthymides is probably also the master of a larger work, a clay plaque from the Acropolis, with a warrior painted part in outline, part in black-figure (*Ill. 92*). Among contemporaries, working on smaller vases generally, are Oltos, a robust, economical draughtsman (*Ill. 91*), and Epiktetos, whose figures are closer to those on the large vases but more delicately conceived. At the end of our period the greatest names (or pseudonyms) are the Berlin Painter and the Kleophrades Painter. The Berlin Painter appreciated the effect that could be made with single figure studies or small groups (*Ill. 93*). His is perhaps the most skilful use of this strange technique which forces all the figures to the foreground, before an inky backdrop. The Kleophrades Painter (we think we

93 Detail from the Berlin Painter's name-vase, a red-figure *amphora*. A satyr is tuning his lyre and Hermes strides past him. The contrast between the intense relief lines and the thinned paint (for the musculature of the satyr's stomach) shows clearly here. *c.* 490 B.C.

know his name—another Epiktetos) lacked nothing in sober strength, but many of his subjects are treated with an originality and verve that we associate more with the cup painters (*Ill. 95*). Of these there are several artists of the first rank working in Athens in the opening years of the fifth century. Their cups are the new, high-stemmed *kylikes* with a shallow open bowl which offered a circular field for decoration within (appearing to the drinker through his wine), and two broad arcs on the outside for frieze compositions which were best appreciated when the cup was hanging on the wall. Onesimos (*Ill. 94*) delicately combined residual Archaic vigour with

94 Centrepiece of a red-figure cup by Onesimos. An excited satyr is squatting upon a pointed wine *amphora*. *c.* 500 B.C.

95 The head of a dancing maenad from a vase by the Kleophrades Painter. She wears an animal skin, painted in a pale wash, over her *chiton* and shawl. A snake winds up one arm and she holds a *thyrsos*—a reed with a cluster of ivy leaves at the top. *c.* 490 B.C.

96 A red-figure *psykter* (wine-cooler) painted by Douris. Satyrs at a party. *c.* 480
B.C. Height 11½ ins

the dignity which is to typify the succeeding period, and which is
especially characteristic of his later work. Douris, a rather finicky
but expressive artist, also had a long career. His vase shown here is a
psykter—or cooler (*Ill. 96*). Filled with wine it would stand in a bigger
bowl full of ice-cold water or snow. The Brygos Painter's notable
output included a magnificently full series of Dionysiac and drinking-
party scenes with shrewd characterizations of drunkenness, excite-
ment or lassitude (*Ill. 97*), as well as more formal mythological
scenes in the grand manner.

97 Detail of a red-figure cup by the Brygos Painter. A bearded reveller is persuading a
girl to come along to another party. The way the eyes are drawn now suggests the profile
view better; contrast *Ill. 88. c.* 490 B.C.

98 Fragment of wall painting on plaster from a building in the Phrygian capital Gordion. Apparently the work of a Greek, c. 520 B.C.

It will be realized that painting is a misnomer for the art of red-figure. There is hardly any colour, and no more variety of intensity in the painting than can be copied in line drawing with a pencil. Euthymides's plaque shows what work on a larger scale might have looked like. The light background would have been the rule for any painting on walls or wooden panels, but virtually nothing has survived and we have to look to the work of Greek artists outside the Greek world—in Etruria and Phrygia (*Ill. 98*)—to get some idea of what contemporary major painting may have looked like. For its conventions it seems likely that it was little more than vase painting writ large, but enjoying the added realism of the light background and the greater range of colour.

There are countless smaller objects, in clay, bronze or more precious materials, upon which the artists lavished their skill. Generally the style and subject-matter of the decoration is as that of the major or better documented arts like sculpture and vase painting, but occasionally the special demands of material, technique or purpose produced original and new art forms.

Figurines in clay, mass produced from a mould and generally painted before being fired, are common dedications in sanctuaries, but they were naturally not accorded any place of honour and were from time to time swept out or buried to make way for more. The same figures, of men, women, gods or animals, could serve as offerings in a grave, toys for children or household decoration. The

99 (*left*) Clay figure vase of a youth kneeling and binding a fillet around his hair. Probably Athenian work of *c.* 530 B.C.

100 (*right*) Clay antefix in the form of a satyr's head, from Gela in Sicily. By this time satyrs are often shown with human ears, but here they are still animal. Early fifth century B.C. Height 7¾ ins

original models, from which the moulds were made, were often fine works of miniature sculpture, to which the decorative figurines which abound on sites and in museums rarely do justice. A different class of figure is the hollow figure vase serving as a perfume-flask (*Ill. 99*). The type had been known in the seventh century and is further elaborated in the sixth. Clay figures in the round or in relief also serve as revetments, acroteria or gutter terminals on the smaller buildings, and some of these are notable works of art, especially those from western Greek sites (in Sicily (*Ill. 100*) and South Italy). Here there was no fine white marble and techniques of minor clay statuary were soon highly developed.

Figurines in bronze are cast solid. Larger statuary, up to lifesize, was being made in bronze by the end of the Archaic period, using the *cire-perdue* method which produced light, hollow figures with a thin fabric. The figurines (*Ill. 101*) are sometimes independent works —votive or decorative—but more often were applied to other objects, especially bronze vases. These were naturally more valuable than the clay vessels, but few have survived. The great mixing-bowls or *craters* had hammered bowls to which were applied cast-bronze figures—the volute handles fashioned with gorgons at the point of

101 Bronze figurine of a man reclining at a feast, from the rim of a bronze vessel. *c.* 520 B.C. Length 4 ins

102 A bronze vase (*hydria*) from Paestum. The handle is in the form of a lion, peering into the vessel. *c.* 520 B.C.

attachment to the bowl, elaborately moulded hoops for the lip and foot, and sometimes relief figures of animals, warriors or horsemen around the neck; but no decoration on the body where the clay vases have their figure scenes. The finest of these bronze *craters* are found in the export market; the largest, and by far the best, from as far away as Vix, on the Seine, where the nearly six foot high vessel lay in the grave of a Celtic princess. Smaller bronze vessels may have patterns incised on their bodies, but their handles are cast, with heads, animals or palmettes at either end, sometimes the whole body of an animal (*Ill. 102*) or of a youth, serving as the handle of a jug. From Egypt came the idea of using a human figure as the handle for a mirror or dish. The ladies supporting the Greek mirrors (the reflecting disks were burnished bronze) are sometimes naked, like their Egyptian kin, in the Archaic period (*Ill. 103*).

In the art of gem engraving there are striking innovations in materials and technique. Harder stones—carnelian, chalcedony and jasper—are introduced from the Near East, and with them the use

115

103 Bronze mirror support of a naked girl standing on a lion, with griffins helping to hold the mirror disk. *c.* 530 B.C. Height 13⅝ ins

of a cutting wheel which managed tougher material more easily and had not been used in Greece since the Bronze Age. Scarab seals become the most popular, the Egyptian form with a beetle carved on the back, the stone being set in a pendant or on a swivel as a finger-ring. It is not wholly clear what the exact source of this new phase in gem engraving can have been, but it seems likely to be the work of East Greeks in Cyprus or some other centre where the Phoenicians and Phoenician art were to be found. The Eastern influence, beyond the material and technique, was minimal, and very soon local schools can be distinguished in East Greece and the mainland, producing exquisite stones of a quality unmatched in the East for centuries before (if ever at all). The idiom and style are wholly Greek (*Ill. 104*), and we soon see groups of Greco-Phoenician gems in which the sculptural skill of Greek engravers can be seen superimposed on Eastern themes. The cutting of dies for coins is a craft akin to that of the gem engraver. Electrum (white gold) coins

104 Impression of engraved gem of reclining satyr with cup and bowl. *c.* 530 B.C. Length ⅞ in

were struck first in Asia Minor and East Greece before 600, and by the end of the Archaic period most Greek cities of importance (except Sparta who abjured this root of all evil) had their own issues of silver coinage (*Ill. 105*). Some of the types are as delicately conceived as those on the best gems, although once a coin device is accepted a natural conservative tendency made against rapid changes of style or type. In this respect smaller States were often able to afford greater variety and originality in their coin types. As on the scarabs, with their oval fields, so the circular field of a coin presented special difficulties of composition which the Greek artist triumphantly faced, as he had done in the *tondo* centrepieces of painted cups. These miniaturist arts can sometimes offer works of major importance, although they are frequently ignored in favour of the more traditional or spectacular subjects.

By the early fifth century all the major arts which are to characterize Classical Greece have been established and the techniques

105 A silver Athenian coin with a gorgoneion on the front and a lion's mask and paws in the sunken punched square of the reverse. Mid sixth century B.C.

mastered. Indeed, a great many of the special features of Classical art, its peculiar blend of idealism and realism, are already anticipated. If the main breakthrough in sculpture is the rejection of the stiff *kouros* pose, then this has happened already by the time of the Persian Wars. Not in the lively poses of relief and architectural sculpture, but in figures like the 'Critian boy' from the Athenian Acropolis (*Ill. 106*), who is still a standing frontal youth—a *kouros*—but relaxed, with his weight shifted on to one leg, hip raised, body gently curved: the work of a sculptor who could now express his understanding of the human body as a structure of bones and flesh, rather than a stiff-limbed puppet.

When the Persian generals left their treasures behind in their tents after defeat on the battlefield of Plataea, those Eastern *objets de luxe* offered no new art forms to excite Greek artists, and soon Greece was to repay in full, and more, its debt to those Eastern crafts whose effect we have observed in the last two chapters.

106 The 'Critian boy', so named from the similarity of the head to that of the tyrannicide Harmodius in the group by Critios and Nesiotes (which is known from copies). From the Athenian Acropolis, of just before 480 B.C. Height 33 ins

CHAPTER FOUR

Classical Sculpture and Architecture

The Persian Wars left Athens devastated, her temples burnt and monuments overthrown by the invader, and although she soon won back prosperity and an ascendancy over part of the Greek world, which she had earned by her stand against the barbarian, the city had for a while no time or money to lavish on monumental art. For the first-fruits of the break with Archaic conventions which had already occurred before the Persian Wars we have to look elsewhere. The great national sanctuary of Zeus at Olympia, unscathed by Persian attack, is the natural place to look for examples of the new, incipient Classical style, and the accidents of survival have preserved here some of the finest works of the generation after the Battle of Salamis. After a flood in late antiquity, which covered the site with a deep layer of sand, Olympia was barely visited, rarely robbed and for a long while lost. From beneath the sand and from a rough, late

107 Restored drawing of the east end of the Temple of Zeus at Olympia

fortification wall has been recovered the greater part of the sculpture from one of the seven wonders of the Ancient World—the Temple of Zeus—and enough of its architecture to admit almost certain restoration on paper (*Ill. 107*).

OLYMPIA

The temple was in the Doric order, and the largest in mainland Greece (over ninety feet long) before the Parthenon, which is some ten feet longer. The coarse local limestone of which it is built is covered with stucco, but fine Parian marble was brought in for the

108 Metope from the Temple of Zeus at Olympia showing Heracles bearing the weight of the world for Atlas, who is bringing him the apples of the Hesperides. Athena stands behind Heracles ready to help to return Atlas's burden to him. Height of metope 63 ins

109 Head of a centaur from the west pediment of the Temple of Zeus at Olympia

roof-tiles and sculptures. The exterior had sculptural embellishment only for the acroteria on the roof and in the pediments—the metopes were left bare. In the pediment over the main entrance in the east the line up of contestants and chariots before the fateful race between Pelops and Oenomaos is shown. Zeus himself towers in the centre, and the corners are filled by reclining figures of local deities. This is a static but impressive composition, only fraught with deeper meaning for those who knew the story. The other pediment has Apollo at the centre (*Ill. 110*), in control but not physically involved in the wedding brawl between the Lapiths of Thessaly and the drunken centaurs who tried to carry off the bride and women. Here all is action, like the earlier pedimental compositions of fights.

121

Passing through this outer ring of columns and looking up over the inner porches the visitor saw at either end six sculptured metopes (*Ill. 108*). These showed the Labours of Heracles, starting with his triumph over the lion, ending with the local episode of his breaching the walls of the stables of Augeas, to flood and cleanse them. Within the main hall (*cella*) a central nave was formed by two tiers of superimposed Doric columns on either side, and at the end was Phidias's great gold and ivory statue of Zeus himself, seated, with a figure of Victory on his outstretched right hand. This seated statue which was said to have 'added something to accepted religion' (Quintilian), towered to the roof. It was eventually taken to Constantinople and burnt in a palace fire in A.D. 475. All that we can know of it is gleaned from later reduced copies of free adaptations of it, and from some of the clay moulds on which the gold drapery was beaten, which were excavated in recent years in Phidias's workshop at Olympia (see page 18). The marble statuary on the temple was in position by 456 B.C., but the cult statue was supplied nearly twenty years later.

It is naturally the style of the pediments and metopes at Olympia that occupy our attention, and which can give the measure of how far the artists had progressed since the Archaic period. Set high on a building, sculpture of this sort is most effective if carved in fairly simple and bold planes. But at Olympia, as on the Parthenon, where the work is far more detailed, much of the subtlety of the sculpture was lost at the height at which it was displayed. For there is considerable individuality and character in the treatment of bodies and features here. Heracles's expression reflects his feelings in the face of his various labours, and in the fights pain and bestiality are vividly portrayed (*Ill. 109*).

The male figures stand in the new, easy pose, with one leg relaxed and the weight of the body lightly shifted on to the other; a pose which marks them off so clearly from the Archaic. The nude bodies are strongly and accurately modelled. A clay group of Zeus and Ganymede at Olympia (*Ill. 111*) shows the new style well, the heads still slightly Archaic, especially in the treatment of hair, but the features cast in a new mould. Another Zeus (or other deity) is the

110 Detail of Apollo from the centre of the west pediment of the Temple of Zeus at Olympia. *c.* 460 B.C.

111 Clay group of Zeus carrying off the child Ganymede, who holds a cock (the usual Greek love-gift for a boy). The bright colours are well preserved on the fired clay. From Olympia. *c.* 470 B.C. About half lifesize

112 Detail of the bronze figure from the Artemisium wreck. The brows and lips had been inlaid with other metal and the eyes inset. *c.* 460 B.C. The figure is just over lifesize

113 The 'Chatsworth head' from Cyprus, possibly from a cult statue of Apollo. Parts of the hair and ears were cast separately. *c.* 460 B.C. Height 12½ ins

fine bronze from the wreck off Artemisium (*Ill. 112*), more than lifesize, and certainly the most vigorous surviving example of Early Classical statuary. This is nearer in date to the Olympia sculptures and shows an advance in the freer treatment of hair and build. Full-size bronze statues of this sort must have been far more common at this time and parts of others have survived. The famous charioteer from a group at Delphi is an obvious example. Another is the 'Chatsworth head' in London (*Ill. 113*), an Apollo head no doubt, from a cult statue of the type which has survived in several complete marble copies.

126

The gaudy pleated *chiton* in which the Archaic *korai* were dressed is generally replaced now by the heavier *peplos*, which is sleeveless and has a heavy, straight overfall to the waist. The change in fashion also offered a style of dress more in keeping with the new spirit. The simple broad folds hang naturally and acknowledge realistically the shape of the body beneath. The *peplos* figures sometimes seem heavy and dull. There is little to show for the style in Athens (*Ill. 114*), where there are no carved tombstones of this date to display the new dignity which would suit them so well, but we may look

114 (*left*) Votive relief showing Athena reading a decree. Her *peplos* has a long overfall, caught in by a belt, in the Athenian manner. From the Acropolis at Athens. *c.* 450 B.C. Height 22 ins

115 (*right*) Gravestone of a girl from one of the Greek islands, probably Paros. The lid of the box she holds is on the floor. Her loose *peplos* is open all down the side. *c.* 450 B.C. Height 56 ins

for examples on tombstones from the Greek islands. Here the narrow type of *stele* with a palmette finial, which had been invented in the islands of East Greece and had been copied by Athens in the sixth century, was still being made (*Ill. 115*). The islands, a source of fine statuary marble even after the resources of Athens' Mount Pentelikon had been realized and exploited, always had important studios, and the sanctuary island of Delos in their midst attracted rich offerings.

By the middle of the fifth century Athens was secure in her position at the head of a large tribute-paying confederacy which was formed to defend Greek liberty against the Persians. The treasury of the confederacy was transferred to Athens itself in 454 B.C. and the statesman Pericles set aside part of the revenue for a programme of rebuilding which was to make the city the show-place of the Ancient World. The construction of temples and public buildings no the Acropolis citadel (*Ill. 116*) and in the lower town went on despite expensive wars in which Athens was not always victorious. By the end of the century she had been severely defeated by Sparta, but the visitor to Athens then would have seen the city at its very best.

The Acropolis, ravaged by the Persians, was completely replanned. Approaching from the west the visitor was faced by a monumental entrance way, in the Doric order, but with tall Ionic columns flanking the central passageway (*Ill. 119*). The Classical approach is still

116 Model restoration of the Acropolis at Athens with the Propylaea and the Temple of Athena Nike in the right foreground, the Parthenon beyond and the Erechtheion to the left centre

11

117 The Parthenon, seen from the north-west, just within the Propylaea. This unimpeded view was not possible in antiquity (compare *Ill. 116*). Built 447–33 B.C., to the plans of Ictinus and Callicrates

that in use, but little obscured by an outer gateway and monument of the Roman period. There is no sculpture here but we can already appreciate the exquisite finish of the masonry, the fine joints, the precision of every moulding which is never merely mechanical, and the way in which the qualities of white marble, be it a plain surface or carved in gentle curves and sharp ridges, are appreciated.

Within the entrance stood the colossal bronze Athena Promachos, the work of Phidias, wholly lost to us. The crowning glory of the citadel—the Temple of Athena Parthenos (the Maiden) or the Parthenon, as it is better known—was not revealed in its full height so quickly to the ancient visitor as it is today (*Ill. 117*), but had to be approached through a second gate and court. The temple, wholly of the Doric order, displays the same precision in the carving and fitting of all its parts as does all Greek architecture of the Classical period. Moreover, it reveals refinements of plan which subtly correct the

129

rather static, matchbox effect of Doric temple architecture. The eight columns of the front, instead of the more usual six, give it an unfamiliar breadth and dignity. The refinements of detail had been practised on many other buildings; a crude early example is the *entasis* of Archaic column shafts (see *Ills. 56, 57*). The same feature, much refined, appears on the Parthenon; the whole platform from which the columns rise sinks in a gentle curve away to the corners; the columns lean slightly in, the upper works slightly out. These are refinements that can be measured and with care observed by the naked eye. It is only when we look at buildings in which they were not applied, or were applied less skilfully, that we can appreciate the effect their absence might have had on the Parthenon's forest of columns and heavy upper works.

The pediments, most of whose figures are in London, illustrated important moments in Athens' myth-history—the birth of the goddess Athena attended by the other gods, and the dispute between Athena and Poseidon for occupation of the city. The massive figures from these pediments tell us how far the sculptors have progressed in their attitude to the figure and drapery in the years since the Olympia pediments. The restless swirl of massed drapery is shown by deep-cut folds which catch the shadows (*Ill. 118*). The material now has a mass, almost a life of its own, but at the same time the forms of the body beneath are clearly understood and as firmly expressed. The wholly relaxed poses of the reclining and seated figures show a new

118 Group of three goddesses attending the birth of Athena, from the east pediment of the Parthenon. *c.* 435 B.C.

119 The Propylaea to the Acropolis at Athens, from the south-west. An Ionic column from the centre passageway can be seen centre right. Built 437–2 B.C., to plans of Mnesicles. Width of entrance front 62 ft

confidence which even the Olympia sculptures still lack. The figures are carved wholly in the round, and finished as carefully at the back (never seen once they were in position on the building) as at the front. The few remaining heads are badly battered, and for an idea of the way heads were treated by this school of artists we must turn to the relief work on the temple—the metopes and frieze.

The metopes all round the outside of the temple were carved, unlike at Olympia. There are simple groups of struggling figures—gods and giants, Lapiths and centaurs, Greeks and Trojans at the sack of Troy, and Greeks and Amazons. Some groups are poorly planned and others seem to burst the frame of the metope. The best are tautly composed and set neatly in the field (*Ill. 120*).

The frieze was set in the same place as the carved metopes at Olympia, that is inside the outer colonnade; but in the Parthenon the relief runs over the end porches and along both long sides of the main *cella*. It is thus continuous all round the centre block of the building. Its subject is the preparation for the Panathenaic procession in honour of the goddess, in itself an unusual, secular, subject for the decoration of a temple. It shows the progress from the preparations in the town, with the horsemen moving through the streets (*Ill. 121*), headed by burghers and attendants leading animals for sacrifice or carrying offerings, and culminating in the ceremony with the goddess's sacred garment, watched by an assembly of the Olympian gods. The starting-point was at one corner (the south-west); the culmination at the centre-east, over the main door. With the pediments so poorly preserved we have to turn to the frieze to judge the Parthenon's art at its best. The set, Classical features are calm and thoughtful, passionless. The artists, who had no interest in portraying the emotions in features, only rarely admitted nuances of expression or feeling. The idealized mortal is near-divine, self-sufficient and above ordinary passions. We say 'artists', for although Phidias may have determined the design for all the sculptured decoration of the Parthenon and may have supplied models for much of it, still he could not himself have been responsible for more than a small part of

120 Metope from the south side of the Parthenon, showing a centaur struggling with a Lapith girl. *c.* 445 B.C.

121 From the Parthenon frieze, west side. Horsemen preparing for the Panathenaic procession. *c.* 440 B.C. Height 43 ins

the actual carving. This was left to other masons, some of them notable artists, for there is outstanding work among the various hands which can be distinguished, but not identified. Where these artists and masons were found in an Athens which for more than a generation had offered few orders for major statuary or architecture remains something of a problem, but the islands' studios may well have been called upon.

The procession shown in the Parthenon frieze did not in fact have as its object the great gold and ivory Athena which was its cult statue—lost for us, like its sculptor's other masterpiece, the Zeus of Olympia, except in reduced copies. The older and more sacred figure of Athena had been kept in an older temple, opposite the Parthenon and this building too was replaced in the new plan by a strangely beautiful, asymmetrical shrine we know as the Erechtheion (*Ill. 122*). Its Ionic order, the fine floral carving on the column necks and walls, and the carved external frieze serve as a foil to the austerity of the Doric Parthenon only fifty yards away. Its most unorthodox feature was the veranda-like porch, inaccessible from outside, whose flat

122 The Ionic north porch of the Erechtheion, on the Acropolis at Athens, from the east. The holes which fastened the frieze figures to the darker backing marble can be seen just below the roof. Built intermittently between 421 and 405 B.C.

123 A Caryatid from the south porch of the Erechtheion. The figure is in London, replaced in Athens by a concrete copy. *c.* 410 B.C.

roof was supported by six statues of women—the Caryatides (one in London, *Ill. 123*). These figures perform their functions as pillars with some grace. The *peplos* hangs close to the body but the flow of the material is broken by the lively, deep-cut folds, in bold contrast to the Early Classical *peplos* figures, and the straight folds covering the leg which is braced to take the weight recall the flutes of the column we would normally expect in this position.

135

124 The west end of the Hephaisteion in Athens, looking up between the outer columns to the frieze over the back porch. In the frieze two centaurs beat into the ground the otherwise invulnerable Lapith, Kaineus. *c.* 440 B.C.

125 Figures of Athena and a Victory (*Nike*) from the balustrade around the Temple of Athena Nike on the Acropolis at Athens. *c.* 410 B.C. Height 35 ins

126 The Doric Temple of Apollo Epikourios at Bassae in Arcadia. Attributed in antiquity to Ictinus, the architect of the Parthenon. Built in the third quarter of the fifth century B.C.

The Ionic order of the Erechtheion offers more contrast with the Ionic of the Archaic period, than does the Doric Parthenon with its predecessors. In the capitals concave channels in the volutes were now the rule where earlier, but for rare and primitive exceptions (as *Ill. 58*), they were plump convex. In the Erechtheion capitals there are even double channels, and the usual eggs and darts between the volutes have a cable pattern above and a floral band (as in Archaic Samos) below. There had been some variety in the bases too, the Erechtheion having a type developed in Attica. The shafts have twenty-four flutes, with flat ridges between, against the Doric twenty with sharp ridges; and the Ionic column as a whole retains its tall slim proportions against the squat Doric, which made it a natural choice for positions where the mass of a Doric colonnade could have looked unbearably heavy.

A visitor to the Acropolis would have done well to save for the end his inspection of the little Temple of Athena Nike, on the bastion overlooking the entrance. It was a small Ionic building, erected over what had become the traditional position for this shrine, a mirror in miniature of the more elaborate Ionic of the Erechtheion. A low stone balustrade surrounded the sanctuary, and the relief carving upon it offers perfect examples of the statuary style typical of the end of the fifth century, successor to the rather heavy and Classic idealism of the Parthenon. Figures of Victory (*Ill. 125*) are shown in a frieze leading animals to sacrifice and erecting a trophy. The thin material of their dress is pressed so close to the body that some are in effect nude studies, the transparency and swirl of the drapery lending emphasis to the form of the body, and not either concealing it or having a mass and movement of its own apart from the body beneath. The treatment of drapery and of the human body, especially of women, has come a long way since the sculptures of the beginning of the fifth century.

Down in the city of Athens there were other buildings which attested the civic pride and scope of the Periclean building programme. Among the temples the Hephaisteion (often still called the Theseion) stands still well preserved, a smaller and less subtle building than the Parthenon. On it, too, there were friezes within the outer colonnade, but only at each end and not all round, as on the Parthenon. One end showed the now familiar fight of centaurs and Lapiths. The view in our picture (*Ill. 124*) is from the angle at which all such carved decoration was seen in the colonnades, as in the Parthenon or at Olympia (for the metopes). It hardly does justice to the proportion and detail of the figures, and the lighting, here facilitated by the absence of the roof, would have been wholly from the reflected light of the bright marble surfaces around: barely adequate by any standards.

As well as temples Athens now reared monumental public buildings—law courts, council-halls and the *stoa* colonnades which provided offices, shops or shelter for the passer-by and which were to become an important feature of Greek marketplaces. Outside Athens the same new trends in sculpture and architecture were observed in other Greek cities, and because we turn to Athens as the yardstick for the excellence and good preservation of its marbles, we should not forget the other flourishing schools in the Greek world.

127 Restored drawing (by F. Krischen) of the interior of the Temple of Apollo at Bassae. The Ionic columns are engaged on the side walls, and at the end stands one Corinthian column, opposite the side door (invisible). For the frieze see *Ill. 128* and the restored cast in *Ill. 6*

At Bassae, near Phigaleia, hidden in the mountains of Arcadia, stood a Doric Temple of Apollo (*Ill. 126*) said to have been designed by the architect of the Parthenon himself, Ictinus. Although intact to just below its roof it was lost to the Western world until 1765. Provincial in position and workmanship, it incorporated dramatic new features (*Ill. 127*): a side door to the *cella* with the cult statue facing it, Ionic

128 A slab from the frieze within the *cella* of the Temple of Apollo at Bassae. Fight of Greeks and Amazons. *c.* 425 B.C. Height 25¼ ins

capitals of unique pattern with high swinging volutes for the engaged columns in the *cella*, and a single example of a new type of capital, the Corinthian. This has small volutes at each corner and a girdle of acanthus leaves beneath. It was more versatile than the Ionic capital, offering the same aspect from all sides, and it served the same type of column and other mouldings, but not until the Roman period did it become really popular. This temple too, though Doric, had a frieze, here running around the top of the wall inside the *cella* (*Ill. 128*, compare *Ill. 6*). The stockier, more athletic figures of Greeks and Amazons, Lapiths and centaurs, are in marked contrast to the Classical Athenian style, but betray characteristics which had long been the hallmark of sculpture in southern Greece. The drapery has the clinging quality we observed at Athens towards the end of the fifth century.

For the other achievements of this high Classical period, we have to turn to tantalizing fragmentary works which still carry something of the Phidian dignity of the Parthenon. After the mid-century Athenian artists began carving tombstones again, generally with two-figure groups of a seated woman with her maid or husband

140

bidding his wife farewell. The unruffled dignity of the Classical convention is perhaps seen at its best on these reliefs. Something of the same quality is apparent in a type of statue in the round, of a mourning woman, which first became popular in the middle of the fifth century (*Ill. 129*). The pose was employed for the figure of Penelope, grieving over her lost Odysseus, as well as mortal mourners. Votive reliefs portray deities (*Ill. 130*), occasionally mythological scenes, rarely the worshipper himself. A different class

129 Fragmentary statue of a mourning woman—the so-called Penelope type, shown with her right arm resting on her knee; the hand would be at her cheek or chin. Found at Persepolis. Greek work of the later fifth century B.C.

130 Votive relief from near Athens. The hero Echelos abducts Basile. The other side of the relief shows a river-god and nymphs, and is inscribed with a dedication to Hermes and the nymphs. *c.* 400 B.C.

of relief appears at the head of inscribed decrees on some of which the personifications of States (their patron deities) seal with a handshake the treaties inscribed below them.

The children of Niobe, struck down by Apollo and Artemis, were the subject of the pediment from some unknown temple. The sculptures had been taken to Rome in antiquity and some pieces have survived. The girl shown here (*Ill. 131*) is a good example of the sympathetic treatment of adolescent form which can be remarked at Olympia. But there is nothing sensual in this treatment, and the sculptor remains less interested in the female figure than the male.

Man was the measure of all things to the Greeks, and the artist's aim was to portray him at his idealized best, indistinguishable from a god. The heroic nudity of the gods, warriors and mortals shown by artists was a natural expression of the Greeks' open admiration for the perfectly developed male body, and would not have seemed so strange in a society where athletes regularly trained naked and in public, and where clothing for men seems often to have been minimal. We make too much of the Greek 'cult of the nude', which reflects rather the popular and uncritical attitude of a hundred years ago to anything Classical, and was encouraged by the Renaissance's often far less healthy preoccupation with the same theme, and its more sensual aspects.

131 A daughter of Niobe, falling, struck in the back by a shaft for which she gropes. Three other pieces from the group are known including the Apollo. *c.* 440 B.C.

132 The lion of Chaeronea, set up over the tomb of the Greeks killed in the battle of 338, where they were defeated by Philip of Macedon, father of Alexander the Great. Height (with base) *c.* 28 ft

133 Marble head, probably from the colossal cult statue of Asklepios on the island of Melos. *c.* 330 B.C. Height 23 ins

FOURTH CENTURY

The fourth century was a troubled time for the Greek world. Athens struggled to regain her supremacy, while new Powers and leagues arose to challenge her position and that of Sparta: first the Thebans, then the Macedonians (*Ill. 132*), and it was the Macedonian Alexander who, from 336 to his death in 323, completely changed the course and climate of Greek life and political thought. In the arts this century saw important innovations and experiment, although still rigidly within the framework of the fifth-century Classical tradition. The ethos of Phidian sculpture pervades still the more sober studies, like those of senior divinities (*Ill. 133*). In sculpture greater attention is paid to figures in the round, and a final break made with the earlier one-view figures in compositions which positively invite the spectator to move around them by the twist of the body, by contrasted directions of gaze and gesture, or by a pose which from no one position offered a fully satisfactory view of all important features. All this lends a sort of controlled restlessness, which is only to break out into near-Baroque abandon in the succeeding period. Drapery is treated with greater skill and virtuosity (*Ill. 134*). The transparent drapery which leaves the body beneath almost naked remained popular, but also admitted in time the presence of the folds of under-garments.

In the treatment of the naked body it seemed that all anatomical problems had been solved and attention could be paid to the quality and texture of the flesh and muscle (*Ill. 135*). This leads for the first time to a deliberate sensuality in the carving of statues of women. At the end of the fifth century Aphrodite could be shown in closely clinging drapery. Now she is naked, and so successful was Praxiteles in his cult statue of the goddess in Cnidus that (in later times) the marble was exhibited under peep-show conditions and was the object of indecent assault (a Roman copy in *Ill. 145*).

134 A nymph from the 'Nereid Monument' (a funeral monument) at Xanthos in Lycia. *c.* 400 B.C.

135 Bronze statue of a boy, retrieved from a wreck off Marathon. It is in the Praxitelean style. The eyes are inset limestone, with glass pupils; the nipples are inlaid with copper. *c.* 340 B.C. Two-thirds lifesize

136 (*left*) Hermes holds the infant god Dionysus. An original work by Praxiteles, which stood just within the Temple of Hera at Olympia. *c.* 340 B.C.

137 (*right*) Seated figure, perhaps a cult statue, from the sanctuary of Demeter and Kore at Cnidus. The head was made in a separate piece of the same stone (Parian marble). Perhaps the work of Leochares. *c.* 330 B.C. Height 60 ins

Certainly a new dexterity in the carving and finishing of white marble contributed to this effect. We can judge it from the Hermes at Olympia, almost certainly from Praxiteles's hand, though no doubt waxed and polished by generations of temple attendants (*Ill. 136*). The relaxed languor of the figure just stops short of effeminacy. The athletic statues of the day present new proportions—heavier bodies, smaller heads. In the treatment of the heads themselves there is the same softening and relaxing of the set Classical features which can be observed in the carving of the bodies, but the conventions of the ideal Phidian head were not forgotten. For deities or figures at

148

rest the convention is a satisfying one. Its unreality when applied to figures in violent action or under the stress of emotion was at last acknowledged. An intensity of expression was realized by sinking the eyes deep below the forehead, and even the more placid figures take on a serious and thoughtful air (*Ill. 137*). This treatment applied to the two-figure groups on Athenian grave reliefs heightens and charges the atmosphere, and for the first time we have studies in grief, conveyed by features as well as pose and gesture. The figures are cut nearly in the round on these monuments, and the deep shadows behind them, together with the more restless, turning postures, enhances the effect of both spatial and emotional depth (*Ill. 138*).

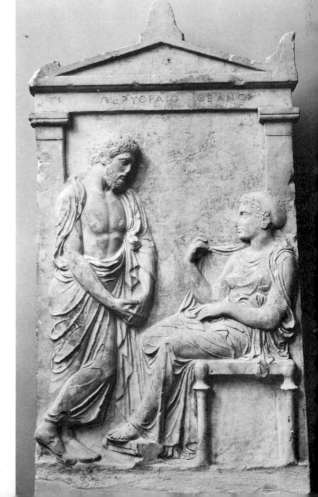

138 Gravestone of Theano, who is shown here seated before her husband. The architectural setting, with the pediment above, is the rule in Athenian gravestones of the fifth to fourth centuries B.C. *c.* 370 B.C. Height 36 ins

It was a short step from this to the representation of more violent feelings, and in an age of great names—generals and emperors—experience gained in portrayal of individual emotions was readily transferred to the problems of individual portraiture. At first the subjects chosen were the great men of the past, artists and politicians. As there can rarely have been any contemporary portraits of them, other than written descriptions, the heads were more like characterizations of a personality in the light of what was known of his temperament and achievements. This almost idealized portraiture remained a feature of Greek work. It tried to express ethos at the expense of realism, where Roman portraiture (or rather, portraiture for Romans, since Greek artists were still normally the executants) sought this end through the more limited, but equally effective means of sheer realism.

On the fringes of the Greek world portraiture of contemporaries was admitted even before Alexander the Great's appointment of a Court Artist for this work. The Carian dynast, Mausolus, had built for him by his widow a massive tomb (which gave its name to all subsequent 'mausolea') on which the King may have been shown in a portrait statue (*Ill. 139*). The sculptured decoration of the Mausoleum at Halicarnassus was by Greeks, and its friezes exhibit the artist's confidence in all variety of poses for men and animals, and a new approach to the rendering of flying drapery which is used to help to bind the whole composition and not merely to enhance individual figures.

ARCHITECTURE

Monumental tomb architecture was still unknown in Greece itself, but there was a growing variety of other monumental buildings, both temples (fewer with elaborate sculptural decoration now) and public buildings. Theatres now regularly received elaborated entrance passages. The stage buildings were given architectural façades, usually functional, for raised stage and scenery, but nothing yet to rival those of the Roman period. Tiers of carved marble seats replaced the bare slopes of the hillside which in earlier theatres

139 Portrait statue of Mausolus (?) from his tomb (the 'Mausoleum') at Halicarnassus. The Carian's un-Hellenic features and wild hair are faithfully copied by the Greek sculptor. Third quarter of the fourth century B.C. Nearly twice lifesize

140 Reconstruction drawing of the theatre at Priene in its Hellenistic form, with a raised stage and panels between the engaged columns for setting stage scenery. The theatre seated more than five thousand

overlooked the flat dancing-floor—*orchestra* (*Ill. 140*). Colonnades and façades are bound still by the Classical orders, but increasing use is made of the Corinthian capital, and interesting new ground-plans are developed. There had been circular and apsidal temples in Greece before the Tholos at Delphi (*Ill. 142*), but here the canonic Doric order of the outer colonnade was answered by slim Corinthian columns engaged on the interior of the walls. Yet another circular building offers an example of the new style in subsidiary decoration —the plump and pithy Archaic florals translated by now into writhing hothouse shrubs at the sanctuary of the healing god Asklepios, at Epidaurus (*Ill. 141*). Among other monumental buildings we find now council-houses and music-halls, *stoa* shops and hotels. The city-states were becoming better and better equipped with public buildings to serve their citizens, while private architecture

141 Carved entablature from the Tholos, a circular building in the sanctuary of Asklepios at Epidaurus. The leaves embellishing spirals and florals are acanthus, which also decorate Corinthian capitals. Completed *c.* 320 B.C.

remained unpretentious; but the day of the palace and luxurious private house was not far off—when new public buildings in old Greece were as often as not the gifts of princes overseas.

Before we leave the monumental arts of Classical Greece there are two other subjects to consider briefly: one concerns the Greeks in colonies, the second, our evidence for the famous lost works of Classical sculptors.

WESTERN GREEKS

The Greek cities in Sicily and South Italy were founded in the later eighth and seventh centuries B.C. They quickly grew rich and powerful, in the early fifth century they resisted the power of Carthage successfully, and they were soon being courted by the cities of mainland Greece for their support in internal disputes. Their

142 The Tholos on the lower sanctuary terrace (Marmaria) at Delphi. Built from the plans of Theodorus of Phocaea, whose book about the building has not survived. Early fourth century B.C.

143 Front of the so-called 'Ludovisi throne', which may be part of an altar. The goddess Aphrodite is assisted from the sea by two nymphs. Found in Rome, the work of a western Greek sculptor, *c.* 460 B.C. Width of front 56 ins; original height *c.* 42 ins

rulers and tyrants made great show in Greece, with their victories in the Olympic chariot races, and no mortal prince of that day could have wished for more.

The outward signs of the wealth of the western cities are the temples they built at home, and the pavilions and presents they dedicated at the major sanctuaries of the Greek homeland. Their architecture was predominantly Doric but it admitted Ionic details, and even sometimes Ionic columns. In the wide spacing of porches and colonnades some of the temples seem to be deliberately planned in emulation of the great temples built in East Greece. The western Greeks lacked a ready supply of fine marble, such as was available in the Greek islands and Attica, and as a result their architecture is largely of limestone, stuccoed over, and they paid more attention to major sculpture in clay. But some marble was imported from Greece and important works were executed by local artists (*Ill. 143*). Indeed, there is also record in ancient authors of Greek artists emigrating to the western colonies. The style of their work is generally conservative and often lacks the delicacy of treatment which we observe in Greece itself. The Archaic conventions of dress and features died hard and the severe style of the first half of the fifth century lingered on. The full Classical style is poorly represented. Our main interest in the art of the western Greeks lies in the fact that it was their rather provincial versions of Greek art that had a profound effect on their immediate neighbours, the Etruscans and Romans.

COPIES

The account of Classical sculpture given above is based primarily on the preserved original works and the evidence of date given by style, context or inscriptional authority. Few statues have survived which either carry their artist's signature or can be identified in the references of any ancient author who names the artist. But we know the names of the great men whose work set new standards for their contemporaries. They are preserved in the writings of scholars, encyclopaedists and travellers of the Roman period. These writers often describe the most famous and influential works, and it has sometimes proved possible to recognize surviving copies of these statues, which had been made for Roman patrons and others while the original work still stood. Comparing copies of the same work, and on rare occasions comparing copies with originals, we can see that many were probably most accurate, lacking only the artist's touch in the final carving of details and features, and sometimes adapted in pose or expression by the copyist. Another difference, readily recognized in marble copies of bronzes, is the addition of struts and supports (like tree-trunks) which were unnecessary to a bronze original.

With the help of these copies of works whose artists are named we are able to associate with individuals and schools some of the innovations observed in the surviving series of originals. This is their main, perhaps their only value, and for this purpose some are illustrated here. But it would be wrong to dwell too earnestly on details of carving which may be far from their model.

156

144 Copy of the Doryphorus of Polyclitus, a youth shouldering a spear. In this successor to the *kouros* type the weight of the body is now carried wholly on one leg. The tree-trunk and strut are copyist's additions. The original was of *c.* 440 B.C. Height 83½ ins

It is comforting to attach names to periods and styles, and to individual works. From the copies of Myron's Discobolus and his group of Athena and Marsyas we can see that he contributed much to the development of the full Classical style after the comparative severities of Olympia and other work of just after the Persian Wars. Phidias's guiding hand may be read into surviving statuary from the Parthenon, but in copies of other statues by him we may judge better his personal style and glimpse a shadow of the majesty of his finest lost works, the great gold and ivory cult statues. Polyclitus's new canon of proportions and model for stocky athleticism is preserved in copies of his Doryphorus (*Ill. 144*). This seems to represent a conscious effort to supply a properly worked out canon for the representation of the male body, and the artist wrote a book about it. Another story, about a competition between famous artists at Ephesus, enables scholars to dispute the attribution of differing copies of wounded Amazons to Phidias, Polyclitus, Cresilas or Phradmon. Alcamenes's Aphrodite in the Gardens may have been one of the earliest statues to wear the exaggeratedly transparent drapery. What we think to see of Praxiteles's style in the surviving Hermes of Olympia (see *Ill. 136*) is confirmed by the other statues attributed to him and of which copies exist. His naked Aphrodite for Cnidus was copied time and again (*Ill. 145*), but it is hard to see beyond the copies what there was to their original which made it so famous, apart from its suggestive near nudity. Scopas's style seems to have been more vigorous and work from his hand may be preserved in fragments from the Temple of Tegea. We can judge something of his style—the intensity of expression and swirling compositions which look forward to Hellenistic statuary—in copies of works like his Dancing Maenad or Meleager. In copies of Lysippus's statues (*Ill. 146*) we have the new, fourth-century, canons of proportion for the human body, and we can also judge how much Alexander's favourite artist did to break with the one-view frontality of most Classical statuary. We learn too that Lysippus and his brother were the first to use casts from life in their studio. These are all names and facts which lend life to a subject which seems beset with anonymity, but they are the trappings only, and our conception

145 Copy of the Cnidian Aphrodite by Praxiteles. The goddess is shown leaving her bath. Her modest gesture recalls that of display made by the seventh-century Astarte-Aphrodite figures. The original was of *c.* 340 B.C.

146 Copy of the Apoxyomenus by Lysippus. The young athlete is scraping the oil from his forearm with a strigil. Once wrongly restored with a dice in his outstretched hand following a misreading of Pliny. The original is of *c.* 320 B.C.

of Classical statuary must be gained from what has survived, with or without an artist's name, and not from the copies. Yet Greek sculpture is still often taught with reference primarily to ancient texts and Roman copies, and it is not surprising that many people remain unaware of its quality until they are faced by original works, and until the postcard views of the copyists' gods, heroes and girlies have been set aside.

CHAPTER FIVE

Other Arts in Classical Greece

There is no one art in Classical Greece that is without its master-pieces, and if we have dwelt upon sculpture and architecture it is because it was these monumental arts which had the more profound influence on the later development of Western art. Despite the individual brilliance of particular sculptors, painters, engravers, jewellers and workers in bronze and clay, there is still an over-riding unity in style which informs the work of each generation in whatever material and whatever size. This might not seem so surprising in such a small country, but we have to remember too the many different artistic centres and the intensive activity of the artists. The display of dedications in the great national sanctuaries may of course have contributed to this unity, but it is more difficult to distinguish the works of different schools in the fifth and fourth centuries of Greece than to distinguish the paintings of Cinquecento Florentines and Venetians.

CLAY FIGURINES

The correspondence between a major and a (miscalled) minor art is well illustrated by the clay figurines which so closely match the larger works in marble. There were, in fact, also some large clay sculptures in Greece, but these represent a legacy of Archaic practice and are not common. The smaller clay works are found still as offerings—standing or seated figures of worshippers or divinities, and beside them more original studies of mortals or animals, the sort of thing that was probably becoming more common in the house as well as serving as a dedication in grave or sanctuary. Hollow masks, intended to hang from the wall, were another form of clay votive, and we see them shown on vases hanging, for example, by a bronze sculptor's furnace, to solicit divine protection for the firing. In the later fifth and fourth centuries the small clay figures offer a

147 Clay figure of a dancing maenad wearing a fawn-skin over her dress and holding a tambourine.. From Locri, South Italy. *c.* 400 B.C. Height 7½ ins

148 A clay plaque from Locri. It shows Aphrodite in a chariot, with Hermes just mounting. The chariot is drawn by Eros and Psyche (?) carrying a cock and a perfume-flask (*alabastron*). *c.* 460 B.C. Height 9 ins

variety of subjects which the sculptor generally ignored. Of particular importance are figures of actors (*Ill. 149*), which can tell us much about the dress and masks worn on the Athenian stage. Beside them are graceful genre studies of dancers (*Ill. 147*) and women at ease or in their best dresses, such as are to become characteristic of the succeeding Hellenistic period (see *Ills. 212, 214, 215*). The

163

149 Clay group of actors dressed as an old woman and a man. They wear masks and the man has the usual comic costume of padded tunic, phallus and tights. Mid fourth century B.C.

western Greeks were particularly adept at preparing fine moulds for such figures, and they also provide examples of a different sort of votive, the clay relief plaque. Locri, in South Italy, has yielded an important series of Early Classical plaques with ritual scenes (*Ill. 148*). There are others from Tarentum, while in the Greek homeland the island of Melos produced a notable series of cut-out plaques showing mythological scenes. Later on we find gilt clay *appliqués* used in various parts of the Greek world to decorate wooden boxes and coffins.

164

Coroplast and vase painter often collaborated in figure vases. These are usually elaborate cups, in the form of human or grotesque heads, or sometimes of more complicated groups (*Ill. 150*). The animal-head cups copy a familiar Eastern form, and there are clay versions of the more expensive metal cups in this shape, either painted or in relief (*Ill. 151*). Some of these are not simple cups but *rhyta*—pourers—for their mouths are pierced. This is a version of an Eastern type of ritual vase, and there are also many examples in which the drinking-horn shape is closely followed.

150 Clay vase in the form of a Negro boy attacked by a crocodile. The neck was painted with satyrs and maenads, in the manner of the Sotades Painter. *c.* 460 B.C. Height 9½ ins

151 Clay cup in the form of a sheep's head. The relief group on the neck shows a fight between a griffin and an Amazon, probably copied from a metal relief. Made in South Italy. Fourth century B.C.

Decorative bronze-work in relief was more often now cast, the linear details being incised on, and occasionally patches of precious metal inlaid. This sort of work at times produced figures in exceptionally high relief and most delicately modelled. It appears on vases but on other objects too—the cheek-pieces of helmets, belt-clasps, and the folding backs of circular mirrors (*Ill. 152*). The reflecting surface of the mirror was a bright, polished bronze, and this may remind us that all ancient bronzes, fresh from the artist's studio, had this bright appearance, far warmer and more realistic than the dark patina of age or the chocolate-coloured surface produced by some modern cleaning methods. Incised lines would stand out black on

152 Bronze mirror-cover with relief scene of the drunken Heracles attacking the priestess Auge. Fourth century B.C.

153 Gilt bronze mirror-cover, with incised design of Aphrodite teaching Eros
how to shoot. Fourth century B.C.

the light surface, and there is an important class of mirror-covers with
incised scenes only upon them (*Ill. 153*), which were as popular as
those with reliefs.

The practice of casting handles and decorative attachments for
bronze vases continued from the Archaic period, with less variety
of subject than hitherto; sirens adorn handle bases, heads their tops.

Occasionally figures in the round appear on the lip or shoulder (*Ill. 154*) of the larger vases—another Archaic practice; or a whole relief group is fastened on the body of the vase beneath the handle. The figures of women supporting mirror-disks survive also, and in the details of their hair and drapery they follow closely the patterns of contemporary sculpture (*Ill. 155*). They often stand on neat,

154 Detail of reclining satyr from the shoulder of a large bronze *crater*, the body of which is decorated in relief with Dionysiac scenes. Found in 1962 in a tomb at Derveni in Macedonia, where it served as an urn for the ashes. It also contained a gold coin of Philip II. Late fourth century B.C.

155 Bronze mirror-support. The woman is wearing a *chiton* and pointed slippers. She stands on a stool with animal's legs. Early fifth century B.C. Height 9½ ins

folding stools, while figures of Eros fuss around their heads, and tiny animals and florals run over the attachment to the disk and around it. This sort of finicky embellishment is not much to modern taste nor easily reconciled with the popular idea of Classical simplicity. In the free-standing statuettes of bronze we also see a greater variety of figures—athletes (*Ill. 156*), deities (*Ill. 157*), dancers. In

156 Bronze figure of an armed runner (*hoplitodromos*). He is in the usual Greek starting position, with one foot only slightly in advance of the other. *c.* 480 B.C. Height 6½ ins

157 Bronze statuette of Pan from Arcadia. He stands shading his eyes. Mid fifth century B.C. Height 3⅝ ins

much of this sort of work we begin to feel perhaps for the first time in the history of Greek art, that the artist is producing an object which has no function but to please mortal eyes (*Ill. 158*), something which is more than a decorative addition to an implement or article of toilet, more than a proud expression of wealth or piety in a god's shrine.

Major works of bronze sculpture have to be discussed in terms of contemporary marble sculpture. Pitifully few pieces have survived but enough to show that, for all the technical differences, there were no very distinct idioms for work in bronze rather than marble. The big statues were cast hollow, by the *cire-perdue* method, as were the larger statuettes; the other bronzes we have mentioned were cast solid.

172

158 Bronze figure of a naked girl from Verroia in Macedonia. Late fifth century B.C. Height 10 ins

Precious metals were used for the smaller vessels, especially with hammered or cast relief decoration. A special class is formed by *phialae*, shallow bowls with small round centres (navels—*mesomphalic*) beneath which the fingers would fit (*Ill. 159*). From representations on vases we see that they were particularly used for pouring libations, and at an earlier date, at Perachora, bronze *phialae* seem to have been thrown into a lake and oracles taken from their behaviour—sink or swim. The jeweller had mastered the arts of filigree and granulation (*Ills. 160, 161*), and occasionally now inlays of coloured stones or enamel are to be found. Signet-rings of solid bronze, silver or gold become common for the first time in the fifth

159 Gold *phiale* from a Scythian tomb at Kul Oba in South Russia. The basic floral pattern is covered with heads of gorgons, men and animals, while dolphins and fish encircle the central 'navel'. The same tomb held the ivory plaques, see *Ill. 164*. Fourth century B.C.

160 Pair of gold ear-rings from Tarentum with wire and granulation patterns on the disks and pendant heads of women. Fourth century B.C. Height 2⅜ ins; diam. of disk ⅞ in

century. Common devices on them are of women, seated or standing, with wreaths or a tiny Eros, or of Victories (*Nikai*). They were probably as much decorative as personal seals. Impressions from them are commonly found on clay loom-weights. They may have been more popularly worn by women, but it is odd that they are not worn by any of the figures shown on contemporary vases, which otherwise give us vivid details of dress, jewellery and furniture.

Engraved gem stones could also be set on swivels and worn as finger-rings, or be worn as pendants on necklaces or wristlets. Only towards the end of the Classical period do we find beginning the practice of setting an engraved stone immovably in a metal ring. The scarab-beetle form of seal remained popular for a while after the Archaic period, but was generally replaced by the plainer scaraboid form with a domed back. The stone is usually larger

161 Part of a gold diadem from near Tarentum with floral scrolls in relief. Fourth century B.C.

now—of chalcedony or white jasper, and the subjects are somewhat more limited. Studies of seated women and of animals are particularly common. Few artists' signatures are preserved, but we know one, Dexamenos of Chios, who towards the end of the fifth century cut a brilliant portrait head and some sensitive and detailed studies of birds (*Ill. 162*) and horses. Gem stones of this type were popular all over the Persian Empire, and there is a large class, made in the East, which owes as much to Greek as to Eastern models. The arts of the Persian, Achaemenid Empire, give us a further glimpse of the return current of ideas and art forms, from west to east.

162 Flying heron on a chalcedony gem signed by Dexamenos of Chios. Late fifth century B.C. Width ⅝ in

The related art of the engraver of metal dies from which silver coins were struck flourished beside that of the gem engraver (*Ill. 163*). Sometimes we know that the same artists were involved (Phrygillos at Syracuse), and often we may suspect it, but there are more signed coin dies than signed gems. In the heads of deities and, later, of princes and kings, which appear on many coins we see a fully sculptural style and often unusually high relief—a positive disadvantage in objects so much handled and so easily rubbed, and particularly unfortunate when frontal heads were attempted. There is a great variety of animal studies too—greater than that offered by gems because coins were mass produced and more different types have survived, while each gem was a unique creation. Conservatism dictated the devices on the better known issues of coins, which relied on the ready familiarity of the types. But although the devices on coins of States like Athens and Corinth change but slowly, other States issued a succession of types with brilliant and different devices, sometimes with an abandon rivalling that of the postage-stamp issues

163 Silver coins. One, of Syracuse, *c.* 413 B.C., signed by Cimon, showing the head of the spring-nymph Arethusa, and dolphins; the other, with a frontal head of Apollo, from Clazomenae in East Greece, of *c.* 380 B.C.

of some countries today (contrast the conservatism of British postage-stamp types). A few issues commemorate particular events or are at least occasioned by them, and in this way have combined the character of medallions and coins.

PAINTING

Of all the major arts of the Classical period painting on wall or panel is the one about which we know least, although in antiquity it was most highly valued. The names of such painters were honoured and remembered, which is more than can be said of any vase painters. We read of the great paintings by Polygnotus and Mikon on the public buildings of Athens and Delphi in the years before the mid fifth century. These early paintings were, we are told, done in a four-colour technique—black, white, red and brown, and Poly-gnotus especially sought to express emotion or atmosphere by nuances of pose or gesture, often repeated on vases or sculpture (as the Penelope type). To later artists are attributed notable innovations in shading, in suggesting depth and roundness, and in *trompe l'œil* compositions. Of all this we can know nothing beyond the suspected influence of such work read in contemporary vase paintings, and works like the ivory plaques found in South Russia (*Ill. 164*), which were once painted, although now only the incised outlines of the figures are at all clear. The paintings in Greek-built tombs of South Italy can tell us hardly anything of the finest styles of mainland Greece.

Famous Classical paintings were often copied, like the statuary, but the wall paintings of Roman Pompeii and Herculaneum translate their originals in a way that makes it a far more difficult matter to recover an idea of the model than it is with copies of sculptures. There are, to be sure, a few paintings on marble which have survived, but none are first class; also some tombstones prepared for painting by incision and backgrounds rough-picked (*Ill. 165*). Closely allied in appearance, although not in technique, must be the pebble mosaics (*Ill. 166*) which begin to be seen on the floors of Greek private houses by about 400 B.C. Until the techniques of shading and a rudimentary perspective were mastered both the painted and

164 Incised and painted ivory
plaques from the coffin in a
Scythian tomb at Kul Oba in
South Russia (whence the
gold vessel, see *Ill. 159*). They
show (*above*) women, and a
youth in a chariot; (*right*)
Athena and Aphrodite with
Eros at her shoulder (from a
Judgment of Paris scene).
Fourth century B.C.

165 Gravestone of Mnason from Thebes. The paint has disappeared from the dark stone, but the incised details are clear and the background was lightly picked away. Late fifth century B.C.

mosaic compositions were bound to be rather linear, and so comparable with vase painting. To the rich evidence for this we may now turn, bearing always in mind what we hope to learn from it about major painting.

VASE PAINTING

Persian occupation of Athens in 480 and 479 B.C. drove the citizens and artists from their homes, and when they returned they had to build afresh. Old wells and pits in the neighbourhood of the potters' quarter are found filled with the debris from the potters' shops. But there is no significant break in production or style. The same painters are at work. In their hands the transition from Archaic to Classical

166 Pebble mosaic from the floor of a house at Olynthus in North Greece. This centrepiece shows Bellerophon on Pegasus striking down the Chimaera. Mid fourth century B.C. Diam. 52 ins

167 Red-figure *lekythos* by the Pan
Painter, showing a huntsman with
his dog. He wears the usual light
cloak (*chlamys*) over a short *chiton*,
and a sun-hat (*petasos*). *c.* 470 B.C.
Height 15¼ ins

was accomplished, as we have observed it already in the work of
sculptors. The cup painters continue the tradition of the early years
of the century, but have at last abandoned the formal, almost Geometric fussiness of the Archaic pleats, and zigzag hemlines. The
drapery is shaking out into freer folds. In details of drawing we find
at last a proper view of a profile eye in a profile head. Bold fore-

shortening and three-quarter views are successfully shown and the artist can experiment further with pose and gesture to suggest emotion, and even give atmosphere to a scene where before a simple event was enacted by, as it were, lay figures.

A group of Mannerists, led by the Pan Painter (*Ill. 167*), represent the old guard, clinging still to some of the Archaic conventions

168 Detail from a vase by the Niobid Painter showing Greeks fighting Amazons. The latter wear Greek corselets over Oriental tights and the one shown here has a leather cap. *c.* 460 B.C.

169 The reverse of the name-vase of the Niobid Painter, showing an assembly of heroes and gods. *c.* 460 B.C. Height 21¼ ins

and leaving their figures to act with a stiff prettiness which seems awkward in the hands of all but the best artists. The monumental styles of contemporary sculpture are best reflected in the work of artists such as the Altamura Painter and the Niobid Painter. Their statuesque studies of warriors and women are a close match for the *peplos* figures and heroes of, for instance, the Olympia sculptures, and their battle scenes (*Ill. 168*) must owe much to contemporary

184

170 Detail from a vase by the Chicago Painter, showing a girl playing the pipes for dancers. She wears the ungirt *chiton* usual for such artistes. *c.* 450 B.C.

wall paintings, both for subject and composition. The Niobid Painter admits another feature which must be inspired by wall paintings. He sets his figures on different ground lines up and down the field of the picture in the manner adopted by wall painters to suggest space and depth (*Ill. 169*). The device is not particularly suited to vase painting and the Niobid Painter's use of it is unique at this time, but it recurs on later vases.

The Chicago Painter (*Ill. 170*) and the Villa Giulia Painter offer more delicate and less ambitious styles beside the Niobid Painter's imposing compositions, and the lightest work of these years is that of the Pistoxenos Painter (*Ill. 171*), or the Penthesilea Painter (in all but his name-vase where he crammed a composition from a wall painting into a recalcitrant circle and spoilt the delicacy of his drawing by crowding detail). It is the sorry fact that when the vase painters over-reach themselves in their figure compositions, which are so seldom properly suited to the curving surface of a vase, the quality of their work can be better appreciated in deliberately selected details, or even fragments.

The subjects shown on the larger vases are more often now of epic encounters between Greeks and Amazons, or Greeks and centaurs, inspired in part by contemporary wall paintings, in part by the popularity of myths which seemed to reflect Greek supremacy over barbarians and Orientals just after their success against the Persians. Except for the work of a few cup painters who retain the Archaic manner we miss the fine, though short-lived tradition of

171 A cup (*skyphos*) by the Pistoxenos Painter. The young hero Heracles goes unwillingly to school (he later slew his teacher) accompanied by an old Thracian woman, with tattooed neck, forearms and feet, who carries his lyre for him. *c.* 470 B.C. Height 5⅞ ins

172 A white-ground cup by the Pistoxenos Painter. Aphrodite riding a goose. *c.* 470 B.C. Diam. 9½ ins

the free and original pictures of dancing and drinking-parties which were so popular early in the century. Their subjects may have been trivial but they released the painter from the iconographic conventions of the usual scenes of myth and let his fancy play over poses and situations of everyday life. There was promise in this Late Archaic exuberance of a whole new phase in Greek representational art, but it was stifled.

Wall paintings showed their figures against a white background of paint or plaster. The red-figure vase painter had eschewed the pale background of clay for his outlined figures but had experimented with a white painted ground, such as late black-figure artists had sometimes used. The effect was of course closer to that of

173 A white-ground *lekythos* by the Achilles Painter. The woman, seated at home, bids farewell to her soldier husband. The lines of the body show clearly through the lightly painted dress. *c.* 440 B.C.

174 A white-ground *lekythos* by the Achilles Painter. A Muse with a lyre is seated on Mount Helicon (the name is inscribed) with a nightingale on the ground before her. The inscription above praises the beauty of the youth Axiopeithes. *c.* 440 B.C.

175 Detail from a vase by the Kleophon Painter showing a girl with a jug.
The guide lines sketched on the clay before the painting can just be made out.
c. 430 B.C.

major painting but, at first, the figures themselves were drawn as if in red-figure and masses of different colour avoided. Moreover, the white ground was not particularly durable. The interiors of some cups are painted on a white ground in the second quarter of the fifth century (*Ill. 172*), but the technique came to be reserved for oil-flasks, *lekythoi*, which were mainly intended as grave offerings and so did not have to survive heavy handling or even exposure for much of their life. The earliest, with figures much as the red-figure, and by the same artists, carry a variety of scenes (*Ill. 174*), but by the mid-century the majority are decorated with appropriate funeral scenes showing the tomb approached by an attendant bearing offerings while the dead watch unseen beyond it, departure scenes (*Ill. 173*), even the crossing of the Styx with the ferryman Charon. For these a new technique was adopted. The outline and details of the figures are drawn in mat paint instead of the brilliant black, and broad washes of colour laid over drapery and details. This fully polychrome style is perhaps the closest we come to Classical major painting. The pity is that the white ground is fugitive and few vases have survived in good condition. The Achilles Painter was an important artist of white-ground *lekythoi*, some of them impressively large vases of around eighteen inches in height. The subjects are, in their spirit at least, close to those of the carved grave reliefs, and there are many points of comparison between the vases (*Ill. 176*) and Phidian sculpture or the dignity of contemporary gravestones. The class of white-ground *lekythoi* barely outlives the fifth century.

The Achilles Painter has been named for his work in red-figure— a fine, rather dapper study of the great hero (*Ill. 178*). His contemporaries, of the Parthenon period, include fewer artists of top rank than we have met hitherto. But their work shows the same sort of advance as does the sculpture of these years. The proper rendering of anatomical detail—profile eyes and three-quarter views—is thoroughly mastered. The equivalent to the massed drapery of the Parthenon marbles is, in vase painting, the breaking of the straight or flowing folds into interrupted lines and hooks which suggest the same sort of bunching or broken fall of material. There are still many vases later in the century of worth and dignity (*Ill. 175*), but there is

176 A white-ground *lekythos* (Group R) showing a young warrior seated before a gravestone, with a youth and a girl who holds his shield and helmet. The outlines are here painted in a mat paint. End of the fifth century B.C. Height 18⅞ ins

177 A red-figure squat *lekythos* by the Eretria Painter. A girl is undressing; an amulet is fastened to her thigh. On the floor behind her is a vessel (*plemochoe*) of a type which probably held scented water. *c.* 430 B.C. Height 3 9/16 ins

a marked preference now for either large and showy pieces, or thoroughly domestic boudoir scenes. Both set the pattern for what is to come in the fourth century. We soon come to learn the detail of an Athenian girl's dressing-room, her gestures before the mirror or the wash-basin (*Ill. 177*). The tiny figures of Eros swarm like gnats to adjust a veil or hold a mirror. Even Dionysus is by now a beardless effeminate youth, his maenads are well-mannered dancing-partners, his satyrs sleek gigolos. Landscape is still ignored.

178 A detail from the Achilles Painter's name-vase, showing the hero shouldering a spear. At the centre of his corselet is the tiny head of a gorgon. *c.* 440 B.C.

179 A red-figure *pelike* by the Marsyas Painter. Peleus has surprised Thetis while bathing. The sea-goddess's mutations, to evade capture, are shown by the serpent attacking Peleus. Other nymphs are spectators and Eros is crowning the successful hero. Third quarter of the fourth century B.C.

The transparent draperies of late-fifth-century sculptures are matched by the close-set linear contours of folds which embrace the figures. For the first time on vases, where the nakedness of women had appeared long before it was commonly shown by sculptors, we find a near-sensual treatment of bodies and drapery. The vases of the Meidias Painter and his circle show this new approach at its best (*Ill. 180*).

180 Detail of a vase by the Painter of the Carlsruhe Paris. The Judgment of Paris. The Trojan Prince, in Eastern dress, sits with his dog, holding a throwing-stick, before Hermes. He is being suborned by an Eros to give the prize for beauty to Aphrodite, who sits with another Eros to the right. Athena is on the left and the other contestant, Hera, out of the picture. The bust above is of Eris, 'Strife', for this episode was the source of the Trojan War. Late fifth century B.C.

181 Detail from a South Italian red-figure vase by the Karneia Painter. A girl plays the pipes
for Dionysus. The close-set lines on her dress accentuate her figure. Her necklace and brace-
lets are rendered in low relief. Contrast the rather earlier Athenian treatment of this subject
in *Ill. 170. c.* 400 B.C.

The challenge of major painting led the fourth-century painter to experiment again with varying ground lines, and to attempt a more polychrome effect within the limitations of red-figure, by the generous use of white paint and sometimes gilding. This, together with the more florid types of subsidiary decoration, produced gaudy and ambitious works which seem to have enjoyed some success (*Ill. 179*). It is none too easy to suppress distaste at some of these florid productions, but in detail there is much to enjoy in the extremely accomplished line drawing which some of these vases display.

So far in this chapter we have mentioned only Athenian painted vases. The success of Athenian black-figure, and the new red-figure technique had succeeded in driving the wares of all other schools out of the markets of the Greek world, and virtually all figure-decorated vases used by Greeks are now from Athens' potters' quarter. Only among the western Greeks was there any notable production of red-figure, and this was a direct offshoot of the Athenian tradition. Athens sent settlers to Thurii in South Italy in the mid fifth century. With them, it seems, went potters and some painters, and in the second half of the century we find painting on South Italian vases of a quality which can at times match the best in Athens (*Ill. 181*), although the more lively Athenian styles of the later century are not represented. In the fourth century other schools appear in the Greek or Hellenized areas of Sicily and South Italy. Few are at all distinguished (*Ill. 182*) but the westerners' love of the theatre (and the theatrical) is reflected in a number of large and grotesquely over-ornamented vases made in Apulia (the heel of Italy) and decorated with tableaux representing the action and actors of plays. And from the Paestan studios come engaging studies of a local variety of farce —the *phlyax* plays—in which padded and masked actors parodied the heroic and epic stories which were treated in a more solemn manner by the Athenian tragedians (*Ill. 183*). It is easier to catch something of the spirit of Aristophanes in these later *phlyax* vases than on anything made in Athens.

A similar mocking spirit—and humour on Greek vases is usually hard to seek—is seen in a class made largely for dedication at a

182 A red-figure squat *lekythos* (its lip missing) made in Apulia (South Italy). Aphrodite suckles and plays with Erotes who tumble from a box. Early fourth century B.C. Height 7¼ ins

183 A *phylax* vase. The central player caricatures the hero Heracles reclining at a feast and being served by two elderly *phylax* actors. The raised stage is shown. Fourth century B.C.

184 A Boeotian Cabirion cup. A hairy ogress (? a gorilla) is chasing a traveller, who has dropped his baggage, towards a tree. Two men have already abandoned their plough and taken to its branches. Fourth century B.C.

sanctuary (the Cabirion) near Thebes in Central Greece. For these the old black-figure technique was employed (*Ill. 184*). It had never been forgotten in Greece, and even in Athens it was practised on into the Hellenistic period for the Panathenaic prize vases.

The finer styles of vase painting did not survive the end of the fourth century in Athens. The attempts to imitate major painting could not succeed through the severe limitations of the red-figure technique, not least its black background and essentially bichrome appearance. But plain vases painted with a fine black gloss paint were already popular in the fifth century, as were cups and other vessels with a very simple, but often elegant, floral pattern (*Ill. 185*). It seemed inevitable that these simpler vases would remain in favour for ordinary use while the painters of figure-decorated vases went out of business through the coarseness or over-elaboration of their work. The plain vases admitted simple impressed decoration, and eventually, in imitation of metalware, relief decoration. These are to be the dominant styles for clay vases for many years to come.

185 A Boeotian clay jar (*pyxis*) with floral patterns of the sort met in Boeotia, Euboea and, to some degree, Athens in the late fifth and fourth centuries B.C. This is of the late fifth century. Height 5½ ins

CHAPTER SIX

Hellenistic Art

Deinde cessavit ars: 'then art stopped'. Thus the Roman scholar Pliny recorded the course of Greek art after the achievements of Lysippus, and although he admits a rally after a hundred and fifty years it is Classicizing, and unoriginal. He condemned to oblivion the artists who worked for the Hellenistic kings and who brought to fruition—if not over-ripeness—all the experiments in technique and composition of the earlier centuries. Yet we may concede something if we take him to mean (as he surely did not) that everything achieved by Hellenistic artists had been foreshadowed by their predecessors, since only in certain respects (which we might have thought to have appealed to a Roman)—in realism, the expression of violence, movement and personality—does the progress represent a real or valuable contribution to the development of Classical art, in the broadest sense of that term.

The word 'Hellenistic' was first applied by scholars who thought that the period and its arts displayed a fusion of Greek and Oriental traditions, which we can better now see to be a serious misconception —especially for the arts. These arts of the new age are deployed more for the satisfaction of men and kings, for the embellishment of private houses and palaces, than for the glory of the gods and the State. Even dedications display a degree of pride and propaganda rather than anonymous piety. In these respects at least the political and social climate of the day had a most profound effect on the arts. The change was brought about by the vision, brilliance and ruthlessness of one man.

Alexander the Great (*Ill. 186*) was a Macedonian—only by courtesy a Greek and, in the opinion of his political opponents in Athens, of a race better suited to the rearing of slaves than of generals or politicians. Yet he carried the boundaries of his kingdom by force of arms—of Greek arms—to beyond that Persian Empire which had

186 Portrait head of Alexander on a gem of quartz. He wears the ram horns of Zeus Ammon. Late fourth century B.C. Width 1 in

once threatened to overwhelm Greece. When he died, in June 323 in Babylon, at the age of thirty-two, Greece itself had been united for the first time since the days of Mycenae, and the limits of Greek rule stretched to the Indus in the east, from South Russia to Egypt in the north and south. Only in the west was Greek influence still contained by the power of Carthage and Rome.

After Alexander's death this empire shrank and split, but the pattern of empire had been set, and the country of Greece itself was no longer the only, or even the main, centre of influence and wealth in the Greek world. Alexander's successors created their own, smaller empires, centred in Macedon in the Greek peninsula, at Pergamum in Asia Minor, at Antioch in the Near East, and at Alexandria in Egypt.

The style, scale and content of Greek art had changed profoundly, in ways foreshadowed under Alexander. New dynastic centres promote palace architecture which is Oriental in magnificence and of a sort not seen in Greece (again, since Mycenae). The new Courts acted as foci for artists from all parts of the Greek world, and the new royal patronage had different demands to those of the city-states and private individuals who had hitherto sponsored major works. The great works of statuary now commemorate events like victories in Asia Minor over Gauls, they show the city-goddess of Antioch (*Ill. 187*), new Greco-Egyptian deities, or they are portraits of new royal families. In Greece itself many of the new buildings are gifts of the Macedonian princes overseas, just as later they were to be the gifts of Roman emperors. In the years that were to pass before the Roman conquest of Greece and eventual establishment of the Roman Empire the Greek homeland was to play a much reduced

187 Copy of the statue of Tyche, 'Good Fortune', the city-goddess of Antioch. She wears a castle-crown and before her swims the River Orontes. The original was of the early third century B.C.

part in the story of Greek art. The cities and the great buildings, as those on Athens' Acropolis, had been long established and there was no room for the magnificent new architectural and town-planning projects such as could be indulged in the many completely new foundations which were made in Asia Minor, Syria and Egypt. And even there many of the sites of the older great cities were abandoned for new foundations in yet more commanding positions near at hand—as at Smyrna, Cnidus and the Seleucias in Syria and on the Tigris (supplanting Babylon).

ARCHITECTURE

The great city of Pergamum in Asia Minor and the buildings and sculptures commissioned by the Attalid kings could almost serve as texts for a study of all Hellenistic art (*Ill. 188*). It is still not clear where

188 Restored model of the Acropolis at Pergamum, in western Asia Minor

189 Part of the fourth-century Ionic Temple of Artemis at Sardis, the Lydian capital in Asia Minor. The slopes of the steep Acropolis rise behind it. The fluting of the column shafts was not completed. Height of two columns 58 ft, 2 ins

the earlier town was, but it was certainly not centred on the massive hill which rises some one thousand feet above the plain by the River Caicus and where the Hellenistic kings built their palaces. The crown of the wind-swept rock was laid out by successive kings as their capital. The view we have of it in drawings and models is one never appreciated in antiquity, except by the birds, and we should rather put ourselves in the position of a visitor climbing to its walls, and being presented with a seemingly endless series of terraces and colonnades reaching up and away into the heavens. On the lowest stood an open, colonnaded marketplace (*agora*). The *stoas* flanking it are versions of the buildings which had come to play such an important part in Greek public life—long colonnades with rows of shops behind and often on two storeys, providing not only a market but a shelter and meeting-place (as for the 'Stoic' philosophers of Athens), even a hotel. It was a Pergamene king who gave Athens' *agora* a new *stoa*, now reconstructed as a museum (*Ill. 190*). Above Pergamum's *agora*, in an open court, stood the Great Altar of Zeus (to whose sculptures we shall return), a monumental version of a type with a long history in East Greece—a broad flight of steps rising between projecting bastions to a high flat platform. Higher still stood a Temple of Athena in its own colonnaded court, which gave entrance to the library (our word 'parchment' derives from *pergamena charta*, 'Pergamene paper'). At the top of the hill stood the palace courtyards, barracks, and, later, a temple built by the Roman Emperor Trajan. Cut deep in the side of the hill was the theatre, seating some ten thousand spectators.

The colossal temple buildings sponsored by the Hellenistic kings were anticipated by the rebuilding of the great Temple of Artemis at Ephesus in the fourth century. At Sardis (*Ill. 189*) a new temple for Cybele is distinguished for the elaboration of its Ionic order, notably the capitals. At Didyma, near Miletus, the new temple is in effect a massive screen whose ruins still dominate the Turkish village beside it. Within its open court stood a separate small shrine. The outer columns, Ionic, stood sixty-five feet high, many of them on elaborately carved, polygonal bases. Here too we meet sculptured heads and busts emerging from the volutes of the capitals, and more

190 Restored cut-away model of the Stoa of Attalus in the marketplace at Athens, showing the broad colonnaded walks (Doric and Ionic below; Ionic and Pergamene palm capitals above) in front of the rows of shops and offices. Second century B.C. Length 382 ft; depth (with promenade) 64 ft

sculpture applied amid the usual floral mouldings. The near-Baroque character of this decoration will be met again in the major sculpture of the period.

Apart from the temples and other public buildings we have mentioned there are other major architectural works of the Hellenistic period, including some quite new conceptions executed still within the canons of the Classical order. The Eastern fashion for monumental tombs gained ground. Theatres received more architectural ornament, though not as much as in the Roman period. Less common are buildings like the Tower of the Winds at Athens— a clocktower of the first century B.C.; and the great lighthouse (*Pharos*) at Alexandria, one of the seven wonders of the Ancient World. We know it only from descriptions and sketchy representations of it on minor works. It stood over four hundred and forty feet high.

The architecture of private houses is a little more enterprising than hitherto. They offer more opportunity for painted and mosaic

209

191 A tower in the city wall at Perge in southern Asia Minor. The windows on the upper floors were ports for catapults. Third century B.C.

decoration now and are larger and more sumptuously appointed, but they observe still the common Mediterranean introspective plan of rooms grouped round a courtyard, and there was not usually any exterior architectural order or decorated façade. The appearance of the streets in even the richer quarters of Hellenistic cities must have been as dull and unvaried as Pompeii. In the big and crowded cities like Alexandria we may suspect tenement-like buildings of the sort built by the Romans in Ostia. With the advent of the catapult fortifications become more massive, and where before we may have admired the fine jointing of the masonry, now its massiveness is of more immediate note (*Ill. 191*).

In the Hellenistic period we are happily able to deal still with a large proportion of original works of sculpture rather than Roman copies. Pergamum, whose architecture has already occupied our attention, is also the source of some notable statuary, and, it seems, was the seat of an important and distinctive school. On the Great Altar of Zeus (*Ill. 192*) King Eumenes II (reigned 197–59 B.C.) had carved a colossal encircling frieze representing the battle of gods and giants. The action virtually seethes around the monument with the figures climbing and crawling up the steps leading up to the sacrificial platform. The fullest dramatic use is made of swirling drapery, but the main force is lent by the vigorous carving of muscles and

192 The north wing of the Great Altar of Zeus at Pergamum. The upper colonnade is Ionic. Beneath it and beside the stairs runs the frieze showing the battle of gods and giants. *c.* 180 B.C. Height of sculptured frieze 90 ins

193 Detail from the frieze of the Great Altar of Zeus at Pergamum. A winged giant (Alkyoneus is seized by the hair by Athena. A snake encircles his body. *c.* 180 B.C.

the writing, tense bodies. If this alone were not enough to convey the horror of the struggle the faces too were carved with expressions of extreme anguish (*Ill. 193*). This work of the second century B.C. shows the Pergamene style at its most intense and offers us the full measure of the difference between the approaches of the Hellenistic sculptor and that of his still Classical, fourth-century predecessor. The antecedents of this mature style can be traced at Pergamum in the third-century dedications (by Attalus I; reigned 241–197 B.C.) celebrating the victories over Gauls. One series includes the group of a Gaul and his wife (*Ill. 194*), and the famous Dying Gaul (long

194 Copy of the group showing a Gaul slaying himself and supporting the dead body of his wife, from the series dedicated at Pergamum by Attalus I. The original was carved in the late third century B.C. Height 84 ins

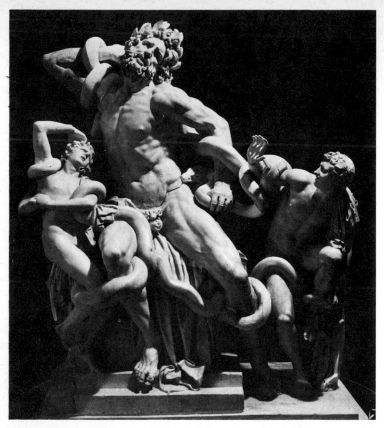

195 Laocoön, priest of Troy, with his two sons struggles against the serpents sent by Apollo. The newly restored group, shown here, has Laocoön's right hand in the correct position behind his head. Signed by Hagesandros, Polydoros and Athanadoros of Rhodes. Second–first century B.C. Height 96 ins

miscalled the Dying Gladiator). The other, dedicated in Athens, is of smaller figures of Greeks and Amazons, Athenians and Persians, gods and giants, and Gauls. Both are known only in copies. The dramatic qualities of the later Pergamum altar are seen already here, together with studies in exhaustion or despair which are not so highly stressed, and so look back to the art of the fourth-century Athenian gravestones. These figures and groups are impeccably carved in the round, and offer many viewpoints. The closely related Laocoön group (*Ill. 195*), which is one of the most famous original works of the Hellenistic period, was designed for a single viewpoint and reproduces all the expressive modelling and anguish of features seen on the altar.

Introducing Hellenistic sculpture with the Pergamene style highlights the contrast with what went before, but does little justice to the strong Classical tradition in the treatment of features and drapery which can be observed in the work of other cities. This seems left to the schools of Alexandria, Rhodes and mainland Greece, but the definition of the styles of these regional schools is not at all clearcut. The all-round viewpoints for free-standing statues which Lysippus had introduced, is achieved by the composition of drapery with folds running counter to folds, even seen through upper garments as though they were transparent (*Ill. 196*), and by twisting

196 Figures of the Athenian couple, Cleopatra and Dioscurides, from their house on Delos. Note the play of folds seen through the upper cloak. *c.* 140 B.C.

197 The Victory from Samothrace. The figure is shown alighting on the forepart of a ship, and was set in the upper basin of a fountain to commemorate a victory at sea. *c.* 190 B.C. Height 96 ins

poses which force the spectator to move around the statue if he is to appreciate it fully. Drapery can even be used to express mood, from the swirling folds of fighting groups, or even flying figures (*Ill. 197*), to the quiet foldless dress of more reflective subjects, like the boy from Tralles (*Ill. 198*). Sheer size was appreciated as never before, and new skills in bronze casting made possible works like the colossal statue of Apollo at Rhodes (*the* Colossus), a hundred feet high. It fell in an earthquake, just over fifty years after its erection in the early third century. More than a millennium later it took a train of one thousand camels to carry off the scrap-metal.

216

198 Statue of a boy dressed in a short cloak. He is perhaps an athlete (a boxer?; his ears are bruised) and he leans against one of the turning-posts of a race-track. From Tralles in Caria. Perhaps first century B.C.

Nude studies of male figures remained the norm for heroes, gods, and even distinguished mortals, but the female nude is also a very common subject. Praxiteles's Aphrodite was famous enough, but the Hellenistic figures with their slim and sloping shoulders, tiny breasts and swelling hips are almost aggressively feminine. The softer modelling, blurring details, such as seems to have been introduced by Praxiteles, is carried further in Hellenistic studies of femininity. The Cnidian Aphrodite was often copied but there are new poses now, as of the goddess crouching at her bath, a type attributed to Doidalsas (*Ill. 199*). In the great Venus de Milo, the new, restless spiral composition is expressed vividly in a variant on the old pose (*Ill. 200*). The hermaphrodite figures offer a mean between the current fashions in male and female physique (*Ill. 201*).

199 Copy of the crouching Aphrodite at her bath, attributed to Doidalsas. The type was often copied in the Roman period after the original of the mid third century B.C. Lifesize

200 The Venus de Milo. The
type derives from the fourth century whence the Classical features, but this is a second-century
version to judge from the relaxed,
twisting composition. She was
found on Melos in 1820 with
other marbles intended for a lime-
kiln. Height 72 ins

201 A sleeping hermaphrodite. Apart from the boyish hips the forms of the body are mainly feminine. Copy of an original of the second century B.C.

We have so far dealt mainly with single-figure studies but far more characteristic of the age are the groups—narrative groups we might almost call them—which tell a story and study the emotions of the protagonists. The silen Marsyas, bound to a tree, waits helplessly to be flayed by the brutish slave who sharpens his knife, watched by a bored Apollo; rough Pan teaches young Olympos how to play his pipes; an hermaphrodite wriggles free from a satyr. The realism of expression and emotion seen in Pergamene sculpture has its counterpart in the characterization of over-developed athleticism (the Terme boxer, *Ill. 203*), wasting old age (the drunken woman in Munich or the Louvre fisherman) and—at last—good child studies (the boy and goose, Erotes). The sleeping satyr in Munich is a fine study of relaxed exhaustion (*Ill. 202*). Its massive musculature, like that of the famous Belvedere torso, reminds us of Michelangelo, and both these works were indeed known to Renaissance sculptors.

202 A sleeping satyr (the so-called 'Barberini faun'). The statue was found in the early seventeenth century in the Castel S. Angelo in Rome, and partially restored by the artist Bernini. Early second century B.C. Height 84 ins

203 Detail of a bronze statue of a seated boxer. The brutalized features, broken nose and
cauliflower ears are carefully observed. Made by Apollonius of Athens. Second century B.C.

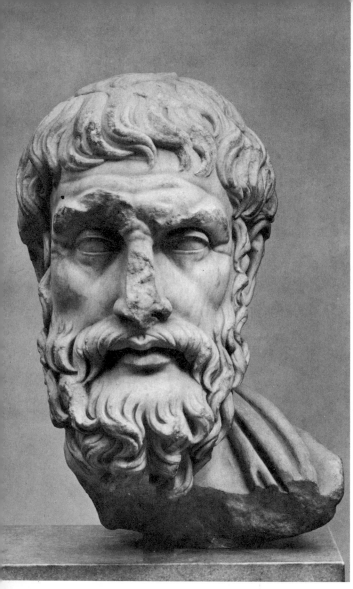

204 Copy of a portrait
head of the philosopher
Epicurus. After an original
of the third century B.C.
Height 15⅞ ins

Portraiture is very much in the spirit of the age, heralded by
Alexander's appointment of Lysippus as Court Artist, the only one
allowed to carve portraits of the King. Portraits of poets, philosophers
(*Ill. 204*) and statesmen remain largely character studies. Portrait
types of Socrates are instructive in this respect. There are two fourth-
century types, one a fairly simple portrait of an elderly snub-nosed

205 Copy of a portrait statue of the orator and statesman Demosthenes. The original, by Polyeuktos, was carved about 280 B.C. The figure is sometimes wrongly restored with a scroll in the hands

man, the other (probably Lysippus's creation) a highly idealized version of the great philosopher. The Hellenistic type shows him rather as the bitter, hen-pecked intellectual. The treatment of the whole figure plays its part in the characterization, even of contemporaries—the statesman Demosthenes (*Ill. 205*) in pensive mood, obese seated philosophers, surly open-air athletic rulers. We do not

206 Detail of a bronze portrait statue of a prince, thought to be Demetrius I of Syria. Rather more than lifesize. Second century B.C.

207 Bronze portrait head of a man from Delos. *c.* 100 B.C. Height 13 ins

know who the figure in *Ill. 206* was, but may doubt whether he often appeared naked in public. The unruly hair, heavy furrowed brow and disdainful mouth are abetted by the massive and proudly displayed body in this study of princely arrogance. This attention to the character of the sitter, making a portrait compromise between realism and an idealized study of statesmanship or intellectual power is the hallmark of the Greek portrait (*Ill. 207*); beside them the portraits of the Roman period are more like effigies.

227

208 Votive relief showing the deification of Homer, who is being crowned in the lowest register, greeted by actors and others. Above are the Muses and other deities, while to the right is the statue of a poet, possibly the epic poet, Apollonius of Rhodes. Second century B.C. Height 45 ins

The most notable works of relief sculpture are to be found now only on funeral monuments. The fine series of Athenian gravestones had been stopped by an anti-luxury decree passed by Demetrius of Phaleron, some time between 317 and 307 B.C. We look now rather to the marble sarcophagi, generally made in the eastern Hellenistic kingdoms, on which whole friezes or single figures are shown in an architectural setting. The spirited scenes on works like the so-called 'Alexander sarcophagus' (*Ill. 210*) bring us closest to the architectural reliefs of earlier years. The tradition of the Classical gravestone with relief figures is continued only in East Greece, but there are many new varieties of votive relief (*Ill. 208*) being made, including a common type showing the deity or, more often, hero, approached by a family or worshippers shown on a smaller scale. Some of these reliefs admit landscape elements and attempts at perspective by reducing the height of figures—features borrowed, not usually with great success, from contemporary paintings (*Ill. 209*). Sculptural decoration on buildings is now less common

209 Votive relief showing a sacrifice in a rustic shrine. A hero and his consort, their altar before them, are approached by worshippers. By the tree are statues of Apollo and Artemis on a pillar. The architectural frame is usual for such reliefs. Second century B.C.

210 Detail from the relief coffin known as the 'Alexander sarcophagus', from the royal cemetery at Sidon in Phoenicia. Part of a hunting scene with horsemen, dogs and a lion. The colours on the marble are unusually well preserved. Late fourth century B.C. Height of frieze 23 ins

211 Marble funeral vase (*lutro-phoros*) from the cemetery at Athens

although there are notable exceptions, like the Great Altar of Zeus at Pergamum. The arabesques which decorate architectural members, and smaller marble objects like funeral vases (*Ill. 211*), represent the last stage in the development of the old Orientalizing florals, and a style which found much favour in Rome and Renaissance Italy.

The small clay figures of the Hellenistic period offer many ambitious and original compositions in which the use of the mould, or of several moulds combined, lent greater variety to what had become a rather repetitive and trivial art form (*Ill. 212*). The model girls of the Tanagra figurines are deliberate essays in prettiness with their mannered pose and coy charm (*Ill. 214*). It is little wonder that they won immense popularity in the last century and that they were widely (and skilfully) forged or mocked up, with their bright colours restored to them, for the collector's cabinet. They are named after the site in Boeotia where they were first found, but the style is common to all parts of the Greek world, with important schools in South Italy (*Ill. 215*) and Asia Minor. The South Italian schools had always been active and original centres for the production of terracotta figures and plaques. In Asia Minor, though, it is the example of the new Hellenistic capitals and their art which probably

212 Clay group of two girls playing knucklebones, from Capua. Third century B.C.

inspired the new activity. One important class of figurines, best known in examples from Smyrna, copied closely well-known types of major sculpture in gilded clay. The realism of major sculpture is reflected in miniature in the studies of the grotesque (*Ill. 213*) or deformed, and the semi-portrait studies of non-Greeks. Alexandria was a meeting-place of the races, and the Macedonian conquests in the East had offered the artists even more opportunity to reflect on the un-Greekness of the barbarians, in looks at least. Hellenistic (Ptolemaic) Egypt has yielded engaging clay studies of typically foreign faces—Scythians, Persians, Semites, Indians, Negroes. The Negro head had occupied the Greek artist long before, in the Archaic period, when he had used Negroid features to depict any African. There were no doubt more dark-skinned slaves in Hellenistic Greece, and we find more sympathetic treatment of Negro slaves and entertainers in the clay figurines and bronzes of the period (*Ills. 216, 217*).

213 Clay mask of a grotesque head from Tarentum; a type more commonly met in figures from Alexandria in Egypt at this time. Second century B.C. Height 10½ ins

214 (*left*) Clay figure of a woman with a fan, wearing a sun-hat. Traces of blue paint and gilding are still visible. From Tanagra. Third century B.C. Height 13 ins

215 (*right*) Clay figure of a woman from Tarentum. She wears a blue and white *himation* over a red *chiton*. The small head, long neck, slim shoulders and heavy hips are characteristic of this period. Second century B.C. Height 9⅞ ins

216 Bronze statuette of a Negro boy singing to the music of an instrument, now missing from his right hand. Second century B.C.

217 Clay flask in the form of a squatting Negro boy. Late third century B.C.

Hellenistic bronze figurines are technically as fine as their predecessors and offer all the new devices and mannerisms of major
sculpture (*Ill. 218*). There must certainly have been more lifesize
bronze statues being made. Even in the Classical period we hear of
sculptors who preferred bronze to marble but the conditions for the
survival of large bronze works (a disaster like earthquake or shipwreck which removed them from the sight of scrap merchants) have
denied us a full series to study, and we have to be content with the
finer statuettes (*Ill. 219*).

218 (*left*) Bronze statuette of a philosopher, perhaps Epicurus (compare *Ill. 204*).
The figure stands upon an Ionic column. Early third century B.C. Height 13⅝ ins

219 (*right*) Bronze statuette of a god, probably Poseidon striking with his trident.
The eyeballs were inlaid silver, the nipples copper. Second century B.C. Height
10 ins

220 Gold *amphora* with figures of centaurs as handles. In relief on the body is shown the attack of the Seven Heroes on Thebes. From a rich find of gold vessels at Panagurishte in Bulgaria, in 1949. Probably third century B.C. Height 11⅜ ins

221 Lid of a silver box with the relief pattern of a sea-nymph riding a serpent, picked out in gold. Found near Tarentum. Late second century B.C. Diam. 3⅞ ins

Decorative metalwork was applied to the same objects as hitherto: vases, mirrors, boxes. Precious metals suited the taste of the new kings, and the eastern victories and loot had offered new sources. Relief cups, especially the animal-head vases, are well represented, as in the recent find at Panagurishte in Bulgaria (*Ill. 220*). Simple, semicircular bowls of a type which seems to have been developed in Egypt serve as models for a popular clay-ware. More decorative use is made of the colour contrast between silver and gold (*Ill. 221*), and inlays in glass or semi-precious stones are also far more common. These techniques, and enamelling, are also features of the jewellery, for which our main sources are the princely tombs of North Greece.

222 Gold diadem from Thessaly, with a 'Heracles-knot' at the centre. Inlays of semi-precious stones only become common in the Hellenistic period. Second century B.C.

A new belt form, with a false clasp like a reef-knot (*Ill. 222*), becomes popular, and the new ear-rings are plump crescents with human or animal heads as terminals. Gold funeral wreaths reproduce the forms of oak and laurel leaves with startling virtuosity (compare *Ill. 223*).

CLAY VASES

The art of the vase painter went into a rapid decline at the end of the fourth century B.C., but the more simply decorated wares persist in the Greek East, and some classes, like the Hadra funeral vases of Egypt (*Ill. 224*), offer a lively variety of floral and animal decoration. Only among some of the western Greek schools do we find a polychrome style of painting, usually over the black paint covering the vase (*Ills. 225, 226*), which approximates to the new realistic styles of major painting, with their greater command of colour and shading. Plain black vases, sometimes metallic in their shapes and in the bright gloss of the paint, had been increasingly popular in the

223 Gold ears of wheat found in a tomb near Syracuse

224 Clay *hydria* from Arsinoe, in Egypt. An elaborate example of a type common in the Ptolemaic cemeteries near Alexandria. Third century B.C.

225 Interior of a cup from Vulci showing a boy relaxing with a wine-flask, his throwing-stick leaning against his knee. Made in South Etruria (the 'Hesse' group) in the third century B.C. Height 2½ ins

226 A plate showing a battle elephant (Indian), its turret manned, leading a youngster. Yellow, white, brown and red paint is used. Third century B.C.

fourth century. The paint, often miscalled a glaze, is in fact a clay preparation which will fire to a permanent black gloss if the atmosphere of the kiln is changed from oxidizing to reducing, and then back again. The technique of this painting has only in recent years been rediscovered. Wedgwood sought it without success, then turned to imitating the easier dull black bucchero, and making relief vases, the technique of which is again Hellenistic in origin, as we shall see.

Where before the black vases carried slight impressed decoration there may now be white painted floral patterns, as on the Gnathia vases (*Ill. 227*) from Italy, or scrolls picked out in low *appliqué* relief (West Slope ware). This is a style of decoration which must be copied directly from the more expensive metal vases (*Ill. 228*), and an even more direct influence from this source can be seen in the so-called Megarian bowls (made in all parts of the Greek world). These are semi-spherical cups, made in a mould and painted black

227 Gnathia vase, painted in South Italy. The black bowl is painted in white and brown with festoons and a comic mask. Third century B.C. Height 7⅜ ins

228 Black clay *hydria* with a ribbed body and a gilt relief wreath at the neck. Made in Central Italy. Third century B.C. Height 17 ins

229 Clay relief bowl. The devices on it include goats rearing on either side of a *crater*, a Triton and a nymph riding a horse. Second century B.C. Height 3½ ins

230 The prophetess Cassandra takes refuge at the cult image of Athena while Troy is sacked. Impression from a beryl gem. Height $\frac{9}{10}$ in

or brown, with low relief patterns of florals and figures (*Ill. 229*), very similar to metal and glazed cups found in Egypt. Rarely, on the 'Homeric bowls', do we see elaborately composed mythological scenes. There are generally only vignettes of figures or groups in floral settings. The type was copied in the Roman period on the Arretine and Samian bowls of red ware.

OTHER ARTS

Only towards the end of the Hellenistic period are the techniques of blowing glass learned in the Greek world. Before then we find only opaque, coloured glass, moulded, cut or built up in coils, used for small flasks or decorative inlays.

Moulded glass intaglios are also found set in metal finger-rings. The earlier types of engraved gems, set in swivels or worn as pendants, give place wholly now to stones set in rings (*Ill. 230*). The stones themselves are generally smaller, and less well carved, except for some notable portraits. Gold, silver or bronze signet-rings remain popular, often with devices showing women (Aphrodite) or Victories. There is not so much a decline in gem engraving as an increase in production and a corresponding increase in proportion of more trivial works, of a sort which go on being made throughout the Roman period. At the same time a new type of gem cutting is practised—that of the cameo. Stones with multi-coloured layers (onyx, readily imitated in glass) are cut in relief so that different colours are picked out in different strata, generally pale figures against a dark background. The cameos are set in rings or pendants. In the cognate art of the engraver of coin dies it is again in the field of portraiture that the masterpieces are found. Where before the idealized features of a god or local deity graced a city's coins, there

245

231 Silver coins with portrait heads of Antiochus I and Arsinoe III. Third century B.C.

are now portrait heads of princes and their families (*Ill. 231*)—a tacit comment on the decline of the city-state and forms of democracy—and a fashion which has persisted, even for many republics, to the present day.

PAINTING AND MOSAIC

Original evidence for wall paintings is as scant as it was for earlier periods, and what has survived in the way of major painting is either second rate or, we may suspect, untypical. Again, many of the wall paintings in Roman houses may reflect Hellenistic originals, but the nearest we come to the sure handling of light and shade in these is in a fragmentary painted *stele* (*Ill. 233*) from the Hellenistic cemetery at Pagasai (modern Volos) on which the painting of the limbs is what we might recognize as modern beside the earlier outline-drawn figures with their flat colour washes. Other painted gravestones from this and other sites are mere daubs by comparison, and were probably regarded as cheap versions of the carved relief gravestones. The polychrome painting on some Sicilian vases is much in this manner (*Ill. 232*).

Akin to these paintings on marble are some gravestones in Chios (*Ill. 234*) and Boeotia which continue an earlier, Classical tradition, with designs outlined on the polished stone against a roughly picked background. Colour must certainly have been applied to these stones, though it is still not clear with what effect. We find on them hunting scenes and some engaging still life.

246

232 Polychrome vase made in Sicily. A funerary vase probably showing the dead woman. The painting was done after the firing of the vase, unlike that of ordinary black- and red-figure. Third century B.C. Height 22 ins

233 Part of a marble tombstone with painted decoration from the cemetery of
Pagasai-Demetrias, near modern Volos. Third century B.C.

234 Gravestone of Metrodorus from Chios. The first frieze shows sirens with musical instruments, the next a fight with centaurs. By a prize-vase on a pillar hang an athlete's strigil, sponge and flask. The incised figures stand out on the dark, polished stone, against the roughened background. Compare *Ill. 165* for the technique. Third century B.C.

235 Detail from the 'Alexander mosaic', found at Pompeii, showing Alexander defeating the Persian King Darius at the Battle of Issus. Copy of a Greek painting of *c*. 300 B.C.

Apelles was Alexander's Court Painter, famous for his portraits and Aphrodites. Of his work, and that of his fellows, who are often associated with famous sculptors of the day, we can only guess from the accounts and descriptions of ancient authors. But we may be sure that it was they who evolved the brilliant techniques which inform the Pompeian paintings. There will be more to say of these in the next chapter. We get close to the works of these artists in some mosaic copies of their compositions, notably the 'Alexander mosaic', from the floor of a Pompeii house. The scene is Alexander's victory at Issus, the young King storming against the Persian Darius (*Ill. 235*), who is already being cut off by the Greeks whose long spears are seen passing across the background. Bold foreshortening and skilful use of highlights lend depth to the complicated but brilliantly lucid composition. In this mosaic the tiny cubes (*tesserae*) are of stone and coloured glass, a technique probably introduced in the third century. In the capital of Alexander's successors in Macedon, at Pella, the mosaics are done in the older style, with coloured pebbles (*Ill. 236*), and the linear quality of the figures is enhanced by the leaden strips outlining some of them. But the limitations of this technique and the few colours used do not conceal the promise these works hold of the later achievements in Hellenistic painting and mosaic.

236 Pebble mosaic from Pella in Macedonia, Alexander's capital, showing a stag-hunt, with the signature of the artist Gnosis. *c.* 300 B.C.

237 Detail from an Etruscan black-figure vase. The extensive use of colour is characteristic of this class and in marked contrast with contemporary Athenian work. *c.* 530 B.C.

CHAPTER SEVEN

Epilogue

Greek art did not come to a full stop with the Roman sack of Corinth in 156 B.C. The Hellenistic art of the countries bordering the eastern Mediterranean flourished as before, although with less originality and with a more conscious nostalgia for the Golden Age of Classical Greece. We are more concerned here with the way in which this transition to the era of Rome's empire affected the course of Greek art, but we should pause too to consider how far the common idiom of Greek art had already been spread. The least receptive areas had been in Central Europe, where only the penetration of Greek colonies into France and on the shores of the Black Sea had introduced the Greek styles. Only Roman arms could complete the conquest. In Africa, Egypt and Cyrenaica were Greek, and by now the arts of Carthage were more Greek than Phoenician. In the East the arts of the Persian Empire which Alexander overthrew were already Hellenized, but the new Empire pushed farther east and eventually in Gandhara (modern Afghanistan) an important school of Greco-Buddhist sculpture arose which influenced the arts of India and, to some degree, those of Buddhist China.

The Romans were no strangers to Greek art, indeed their own arts were wholly cast in the Hellenic mould. This was only in part due to the presence of Greek colonies in Italy and Sicily and the examples they offered of the most developed Greek styles or provincial variants. For the Romans themselves shared, and perhaps even contributed to, the development of Etruscan art, which is itself the result of the impact of Greek and Orientalizing arts upon an artless people. The Eastern elements in Etruscan art we may ignore. They were as soon assimilated and discarded as they were by the Greeks. The Etruscans learned their arts from the Greeks, they admitted Greek artists to work in Etruria and copied their techniques and patterns. It is in the deviations from their models that their character is revealed, such as in painted pottery, where they show

238 Painting from the Tomba dei Tori at Tarquinia in Etruria. The ambush of the Trojan Prince Troilos is shown. He approaches a fountain on horseback. Achilles is springing out of hiding from behind it. *c.* 530 B.C.

239 Head of Velia, wife of Arnth Velcha, from the Tomba del Orco at Tarquinia. She was shown reclining on a couch with her husband. Third century B.C.

a predilection for colour, and for the more monstrous elements of the Greek animal frieze style which they sometimes elaborated in an original manner (*Ill. 237*). They were good copyists of technique—their jewellery rivals the best of Greece or the East in finesse, over-reaching in flamboyance and showy effect. The figure style, though, is subjected to a coarsening of execution and subject, such as can be seen in Etruscan copies of Athenian black-figure and red-figure vases (*Ill. 240*). Greek mythological scenes are copied by Etruscans, but their context and story are not always wholly understood. This is best illustrated in the tomb paintings, where, for instance, we see the common Greek scene of Troilos's ambush by Achilles depicted with all the emphasis on the wrong subjects—the horse rather than Achilles (*Ill. 238*).

Etruscan-built tombs invited painted decoration of a type not seen in Greece, where this sort of tomb architecture was not at that time known. The painting, at first on clay plaques, then on plaster, was at the start done by Greek artists, then by Etruscans taught by Greeks—as were the vases. They give us an idea, at second hand, of the Greek major paintings which have not survived in the home-land. The native element in Etruscan art never overwhelmed its

240 Etruscan cup imitating the Athenian red-figure style. A man takes leave of his wife, with an Etruscan death-demon in the background. Fourth century B.C. Height 15⅛ ins

241 Marble relief slab from a wreck off Piraeus. A Greek seizes an Amazon by her hair. The group is adapted from part of the composition on the shield of Phidias's Athena Parthenos. Height 37 ins

Hellenic form, and in the rich series of tomb paintings (*Ill. 239*), which continue into the Roman period, we can catch repeated echoes of the new techniques and achievements of the lost Greek works. Rome shared this Hellenized Etruscan tradition, and when her armies gave her control of the Greek world, her generals, businessmen and connoisseurs knew what to look for in Greek art. Many Greek sanctuaries and towns were plundered for works of art which were to adorn villas or temples in Italy. The group of Niobids (see *Ill. 131*) was no doubt loot of this sort, and the statues from shipwrecks were probably cargo intended for a similar destination. But besides these simple acts of theft there grew a demand for accurate copies of the better known masterpieces of the Classical period, and Greek artists were long engaged in producing these copies or pastiches of original works which have not survived to the present day. We have already seen how much we rely on these copies for knowledge of the style of some of the masters of Classical Greece. Sometimes the copies are exactly the size of the original, almost mechanically reproduced by the pointing system. These may be of single figures, or be taken from standing monuments, like the reliefs from the Altar of the Twelve Gods at Athens (see *Ill. 7*). More often a Classical type is adapted to suit the new taste. There was always a market for Venuses, and later some were produced with portrait heads of Roman matrons, flattered by the divine physique attributed to them. Other copies are reduced in size, to statuettes of marble or bronze, or the figures are recalled in cameos or engraved gems. Whole compositions may be broken up into component groups, as in the famous series of reliefs from a wreck in Piraeus harbour showing scenes from the battle of Greeks and Amazons (*Ill. 241*) which decorated the shield of Phidias's gold and ivory Athena in the Parthenon.

There are a few original works which were probably the result of the new patronage. A vogue for the Archaic style produced a series

242 Relief showing the murder of Aegisthus by Orestes. A work of the Roman period in the Archaic manner, or perhaps copying an Archaic original. Height 19 ins

243 Portrait of a man, painted on wood in the encaustic technique. These panels
fitted at the head end of mummy-cases in Roman Egypt. Second century A.D.
Height 15 ins

of Archaistic statues and reliefs which copy the massed folds and zigzag hemlines of the later sixth century, and even the Archaic smile. Some are possibly even copies of original Archaic reliefs (*Ill. 242*). On the freer Archaizing works the drapery flies in splaying swallowtails and the mannered prettiness is a travesty of Archaic precision and vigour.

The so-called Neo-Attic reliefs offered stylish versions of Classical figures—often Dionysiac scenes carved on to massive marble vases in imitation of contemporary relief metalwork. Keats's Grecian Urn was probably an elaboration of this type. Other essays more wholly in the Classical manner offer groups like the Naples Orestes and Electra (*Ill. 244*), where the figures of the brother and sister are interpreted in the spirit of the fifth-century Attic tragedians who told their story, and in a version of the sculptural idiom of the same period. Works of this type are attributed to the school of Pasiteles.

244 Group of a youth and a woman, possibly meant for Orestes and Electra. The youth recalls work of *c*. 460 B.C. but the group is a Classicizing creation of the first century B.C.

245 Portrait head of a priest from Athens. 'Roman realism in a Greek translation.' *c.* 50 B.C.

The stricter realism of Roman portraiture has its origins in the death masks and effigies which Etruscans and Romans alike revered. The actual carving, to judge from preserved signatures, remains largely in Greek hands. If there is anything at all to mark off portraiture in the Greek world from that of Rome it is the continued interest in conveying character, and in the form and structure of the features rather than a plaster-cast likeness (*Ill. 245*).

Painted portraits offer a different problem. Back in the fourth century Xenophon recorded or invented a conversation between Socrates and the painter Parrhasios about whether it was possible to depict character in painting. For painted portraits comparable with the statuary we have to look far ahead into the Roman period, but still to the Greek East, to the mummy-portraits of Egypt. These were enclosed at the head end of the mummy-wrapping, in the position which was usually occupied by a relief mask. The techniques of the painting, the highlights and shading, show no appreciable advance on Hellenistic and Roman wall painting (*Ill. 243*).

261

246 Perseus frees Andromeda from her fetters. The slain dragon is seen to the left. Painting from the House of Dioscurides at Pompeii, after a Greek original of the fourth century B.C., perhaps by Nikias

As with the statuary so with paintings, Roman patrons stimulated a demand for copies of the Classical and Hellenistic masterpieces. We know these copies largely from the wall paintings on houses at Pompeii and Herculaneum, preserved in the sudden deposit of ash from the eruption of Vesuvius in A.D. 79. Where the same theme appears in more than one version, and with but slight variations, we may reasonably suspect that a Greek original is copied. Rarely, too, the subject corresponds with a title of a masterpiece attributed to a famous artist, like Nikias's 'Perseus and Andromeda' (*Ill. 246*). Nikias had painted for the sculptor Praxiteles and is one of the great painters of his age, but it is more difficult to judge the quality of his

247 Heracles, led by Iris, finds his son Telephos being suckled by a hind, before the goddess Arcadia and a young satyr. Wall painting from Herculaneum after a Greek original of the second century B.C.

work from the copies of the Roman period, than it is that of his sculptor colleague.

The landscape features of Pompeian wall paintings probably derive from Hellenistic models—we have already seen their effect in contemporary reliefs. The painted architectural styles, much elaborated by the Romans, may owe something too to painters of Hellenistic stage sets. Hellenistic sculptural styles are reflected in works like the 'Heracles and Telephos' (*Ill. 247*). The subject offers a scene in the life of Telephos, founder of Pergamum, whose story was also told in the inner frieze of the Great Altar of Zeus in that city. The poses, drapery, features and musculature of the figures invite

248 'The Three Graces'. Copy of a Hellenistic sculpture group in a wall painting from Pompeii

immediate comparison with Hellenistic Pergamene statuary. And a yet more direct copy of a very famous statuary group appears in 'The Three Graces', from Pompeii (*Ill. 248*).

These are some of the means by which Greek statuary and painted subjects remained in the artist's stock in trade in the Roman period. Gems, cameos and coins repeated the same themes. The low relief decoration of Hellenistic clay and metal bowls leads directly to the Roman red bowls of Arretine (*Ill. 250*) and Samian ware. The finest compositions on these recall and perpetuate Greek motifs. Similar

249 'The Three Graces', by Raphael, A.D. 1500, adapted from the Hellenistic marble group of which a copy had been found in Rome in the fifteenth century (now in Siena). In 1515 Raphael was appointed Inspector of Ancient Monuments and Excavations around Rome by Pope Leo X. 'The Three Graces' type is said to have served as a brothel sign in Renaissance Italy. Canvas, $6\frac{3}{4} \times 6\frac{3}{4}$ ins

relief decoration, in stucco, appeared on Roman walls and ceilings and this encrusted decoration was to be an important medium for the transmission of Greek motifs—both figure and decorative floral —to Renaissance artists. Fragments of the red relief bowls were being collected and admired already in the thirteenth century, but treated as supernatural relics. It is easy to see how the survival of such works, as well as actual finds of statuary, introduced Italian artists to the great range of Greek figure studies and compositions which they either copied or adapted in their paintings (*Ill. 249*), medallions and sculpture.

Finally, architecture. The Doric and Ionic orders for columns, the details of Greek entablature and pediments remained the canon for architectural mouldings and decoration, together with the variant orders, Greek or Italian—Corinthian, Composite, Tuscan. Only in their structural methods—which lie as close to the heart of good architecture as does proportion and decoration—did the Romans add something, in their special skills with brick, concrete and vaulting.

For Renaissance Italy there was of course a mass of Roman architecture available for study, but in Greece too there was much original architecture left above ground to instruct both the Romans and their successors. Italian scholars were visiting Greece in the fourteenth and fifteenth centuries. Many of the buildings had been

250 A mould for a Roman Arretine vase showing dancing girls wearing a basket head-dress (*kalathiskos*), altars, bucrania and swags. Late first century B.C. Height 4¼ ins

251 The reinforced concrete Doric colonnade, erected by the Italians on the site of Camirus in Rhodes before the war, was blown down by a gale in 1961

converted to the needs of a new religion—the Parthenon in Athens; the Temple of Athena (now Cathedral) in Syracuse; part of the Erechtheion ended its career as a harem. Marble is ready fare for the lime-kiln and it is a tribute to the durability of Greek construction and material that so much remained standing for so long— indeed still remains standing (contrast *Ill. 251*). The survival of the physically less durable arts, in the hands of copyists and over so great a period of time, is far more remarkable. It is the mystery and miracle of Western art that Renaissance artists were able to take up the tradition of Classical art more or less where the Greeks had left it in the Hellenistic period, with a spirit and understanding which seem the logical succession to the Greek achievement; and that the main intermediary was the technically brilliant, but monumentally dead art of the Roman Empire.

Chronological Chart

B.C.	Events and People	Sculpture
1200		
1100	Collapse of Mycenaean Empire Dorian Invasion	
1000	Migrations to East Greece	
900		
800	Greeks in North Syria	Minor bronzes
700	Greek colonies in Italy and Sicily	
		'Dedalic' style Monumental marble statuary begins 640
	Greeks in Egypt Greek colonies on Black Sea	Archaic *kouroi* 630–480
600	Sappho, Alcaeus Solon	
	Persians control Lydia and part of East Greece	Athenian Archaic gravestones (600–500) Ionian-type *korai* 560– Limestone pediments Athens
	Pisistratus, Polycrates	'Peplos kore' 530
500		Aegina sculptures
	Persian invasion and defeat 490–79	Island gravestones
	Defeat of Carthage 479	'Ludovisi throne' 460
	Athenian Empire founded 478	Olympia sculptures 460
	Aeschylus	Myron 450
	Herodotus	Phidias and the Parthenon
	Pericles	Athenian Classical gravestones (450–310)
	Peloponnesian War and defeat of Athens by Sparta 431–04	Polyclitus 440 Relief sarcophagi begin
	Thucydides, Aristophanes	
400	Socrates, Plato	
		Kephisodotus 370
	Demosthenes	Scopas 360
	Aristotle	Hermes of Olympia, Praxiteles 340
	Defeat of Greeks by Macedonians 338	Portrait sculpture begins
	End of Greek city-states	Lysippus 320
	Alexander King of Macedon 336–23	Athenian gravestones cease
300		
	Gauls invade Asia Minor	Tyche of Antioch 290
200	Defeat of Macedonians by Romans 197	Pergamene statues of Gauls Great Altar of Zeus at Pergamum Victory of Samothrace 190
	Sack of Corinth by Romans 146	Venus de Milo
100	Greece a Roman province	Laocoön
	Sack of Athens by Romans 86	Copies of earlier statues made
	Foundation of Roman Empire 27	Archaistic and Neo-Attic

	Architecture	Vase Painting and other Arts	B.C.
Geometric			1200
			1100
			1000
		Protogeometric pottery	900
		Geometric pottery (9th–8th c.)	800
Orientalizing	First peripteral temple (Samos)	Protocorinthian (725–625)	700
		Protoattic (700–625)	
		Relief vases	
		Island Gems (675–550)	
		Coinage begins (625)	
	Doric order evolved by 600	Corinthian vases (625–550)	600
		Athenian black-figure (625–475)	
Archaic	Ionic order evolved by 560	'François vase' 570 Spartan cups	
	Apollo Temple Corinth 550	Amasis Painter 550	
	Hera temples Samos 560, 530–	Exekias 540	
	Artemis Temple Ephesus 550–	Spartan bronze vases	
	Siphnian Treasury Delphi 525	Red-figure invented 530	
		Chalcidian, Caeretan vases	
		Euphronios, Euthymides 510	500
		Berlin Painter 490	
		Pan Painter 470	
	Zeus Temple Olympia 470–56	Niobid Painter 460	
		White-ground *lekythoi*	
	Parthenon 447–33	South Italian red-figure begins	
	Hephaisteion 449–	Achilles Painter 440	
	Apollo Temple Bassae 425		
Classical	(first Corinthian capital)	Dexamenos	
	Propylaea Athens 437–32	Pebble mosaics begin	
	Erechtheion 421–05	Meidias Painter 410	400
	Asklepios Temple Epidaurus 380		
	Apollo Temple Delphi 366–26		
	Artemis Temple Ephesus rebuilt 356–	Boeotian Cabirion vases (4th–3rd c.)	
	Mausoleum Halicarnassus 350		
	Apollo Temple Didyma 313–	Original of 'Alexander mosaic'	
		End of red-figure vases	300
		Tanagra figurines	
		Gnathia vases (4th–3rd c.)	
		Hadra vases	
		Megarian relief bowls (3rd–2nd c.)	200
Hellenistic	Stoa of Attalus Athens 150		
			100

The floruits of artists and approximate dates for works of art are given.

Selected Bibliography

General

BEAZLEY, J. D. and ASHMOLE, B. *Greek Sculpture and Painting* Cambridge, 1932

BIEBER, M. *A History of the Greek and Roman Theater* Princeton, 1961

BOARDMAN, J. *The Greeks Overseas* Harmondsworth, 1964

BURN, A. R. *The Lyric Age of Greece* London, 1960

CLARK, K. *The Nude* London, 1957

COOK, R. M. *The Greeks till Alexander* London, 1961

DUNBABIN, T. J. *The Western Greeks* Oxford, 1948

GRANT, M. (ed.) *The Birth of Western Civilisation* London, 1964

HAMMOND, N. G. L. *A History of Greece to 322 B.C.* Oxford, 1959

RICHTER, G. M. A. *Archaic Greek Art* Oxford, 1949

RICHTER, G. M. A. *Handbook of Greek Art* London, 1959

ROSE, H. J. *Handbook of Greek Mythology* London, 1960

STARR, C. G. *The Origins of Greek Civilisation* New York, 1961

Sculpture

BIEBER, M. *The Sculpture of the Hellenistic Age* New York, 1954

BLÜMEL, C. *Greek Sculptors at work* London, 1955

BUSCHOR, E. *Altsamische Standbilder*; i–iv Berlin, 1934–61

CASSON, S. *The Technique of Early Greek Sculpture* Oxford, 1933

CORBETT, P. E. *The Sculpture of the Parthenon* Harmondsworth, 1959

JOHANSEN, F. *The Attic Grave Reliefs* Copenhagen, 1951

LAWRENCE, A. W. *Later Greek Sculpture* London, 1927

LAWRENCE, A. W. *Classical Sculpture* London, 1928

LIPPOLD, G. *Griechische Plastik* Munich, 1950

LULLIES, R. and HIRMER, M. *Greek Sculpture* London, 1960

PAYNE, H. and YOUNG, G. M. *Archaic Marble Sculpture from the Acropolii* London, 1950

PICARD, C. *La Sculpture*; i–iv Paris, 1935–63

RICHTER, G. M. A. *The Sculpture and Sculptors of the Greeks* Oxford, 1950

RICHTER, G. M. A. *Three Critical Periods in Greek Sculpture* Oxford, 1951

RICHTER, G. M. A. *Kouroi: Archaic Greek Youths* London, 1960

RICHTER, G. M. A. *The Archaic Gravestones of Attica* London, 1961

Architecture

BERVE, H., GRUBEN, G. and HIRMER, M. *Greek Temples, Theatres and Shrines* London, 1963

DINSMOOR, W. B. *The Architecture of Ancient Greece* London, 1950

HILL, I. T. *The Ancient City of Athens* London, 1953

LAWRENCE, A. W. *Greek Architecture* Harmondsworth, 1957

WYCHERLEY, R. E. *How the Greeks built cities* London, 1962

Painting

ARIAS, P., HIRMER, M., SHEFTON, B. B. *A History of Greek Vase Painting* London, 1961

BEAZLEY, J. D. *Attic White Lekythoi* London, 1938

BEAZLEY, J. D. *Potter and Painter in Ancient Athens* London, 1944

BEAZLEY, J. D. *The Development of Attic Black Figure* Berkeley, 1951

BEAZLEY, J. D. *Attic Black Figure Vase Painters* Oxford, 1956

BEAZLEY, J. D. *Attic Red Figure Vase Painters* Oxford, 1963

COOK, R. M. *Greek Painted Pottery* London, 1960

DESBOROUGH, V. R. d'A. *Protogeometric Pottery* Oxford, 1952

HASPELS, E. *Attic Black figured Lekythoi* Paris, 1936

PAYNE, H. *Necrocorinthia* Oxford, 1931

PFUHL, E. *Malerei und Zeichnung der Griechen* Munich, 1923

RICHTER, G. M. A. *Attic Red Figure Vases: a Survey* New Haven, 1958

RICHTER, G. M. A. and MILNE, M. J. *Shapes and Names of Athenian Vases* New York, 1935

ROBERTSON, C. M. *Greek Painting* Geneva, 1959

RUMPF, A. *Chalkidische Vasen* Berlin, 1927

RUMPF, A. *Malerei und Zeichnung* Munich, 1953

Other Arts

A Guide to the Principal Coins of the Greeks London, British Museum, 1959

BEAZLEY, J. D. *The Lewes House Collection of Ancient Gems* Oxford, 1920

BECATTI, G. *Oreficerie antiche* Rome, 1955

BOARDMAN, J. *Island Gems* London, 1963

CHARBONNEAUX, J. *Greek Bronzes* London, 1961

FURTWÄNGLER, A. *Die antike Gemmen*; i–iii Leipzig-Berlin, 1900

HIGGINS, R. A. *Catalogue of Terracottas in the British Museum*; i– London, 1954–

HIGGINS, R. A. *Greek and Roman Jewellery* London, 1961

JACOBSTHAL, P. *Die melischen Reliefs* Berlin, 1931

JACOBSTHAL, P. *Greek Pins* Oxford, 1956

KUNZE, E. *Kretische Bronzereliefs* Berlin, 1931

LAMB, W. *Greek and Roman Bronzes* London, 1929

MAXIMOVA, M. *Les Vases plastiques* Paris, 1927

SELTMAN, C. T. *Greek Coins* London, 1955

Peripheral

BROWN, W. L. *The Etruscan Lion* Oxford, 1960

MINNS, E. *Scythians and Greeks* Cambridge, 1913

PALLOTTINO, M. *Etruscan Painting* Geneva, 1952

RICHTER, G. M. A. *Ancient Italy* Ann Arbor, 1955

RIIS, P. J. *An Introduction to Etruscan Art* Copenhagen, 1953

List of Illustrations

1 Athenian Geometric *amphora* from Attica. Munich, Staatliche Antikensammlungen, 6080. Photo: Max Hirmer

2 Marble lion at the Arsenal, Venice. Photo: the author

3 Gilt bronze horse on St Mark's, Venice. Photo: the author

4 The Earl of Arundel in his sculpture gallery, by Mytens. Arundel Castle. Collection, Duke of Norfolk. Photo: Royal Academy of Arts, London

5 The Temporary Elgin Room in the British Museum, 1819, by A. Archer. London, British Museum. Photo: courtesy the Trustees of the British Museum

6 Staircase in the Ashmolean Museum, Oxford. Photo: the author

7 Copy of relief of Hermes, Orpheus and Eurydice. Naples, National Museum. Photo: Anderson

8 Head of bronze *kouros*, from Piraeus. Athens, National Museum

9 Base of Athenian black cup with graffito, from Olympia. Olympia Museum. Photo: German Archaeological Institute, Athens

10 The Lion Gate at Mycenae. Photo: the author

11 Athenian Protogeometric *amphora* from Athens. Athens, Kerameikos Museum, 544. Photo: Max Hirmer

12 Clay head from Piskokephalo, Crete. Oxford, Ashmolean Museum, Department of Antiquities, AE 1102. Photo: courtesy the Ashmolean Museum

13 Athenian Geometric *crater* from Athens. Paris, Louvre, A 514. Photo: Max Hirmer

14 Athenian Geometric *crater* from Athens. Athens, National Museum, 990. Photo: Martin Hürlimann

15 Detail from the last

16 Athenian Geometric *kantharos* from Athens. Copenhagen, Danish National Museum, 727. Photo: Danish National Museum, Antiksamlingen

17 Athenian Geometric *amphora* from Attica. London, British Museum, 1936.10–17.1. Photo: courtesy the Trustees of the British Museum

18 Geometric *amphora* from Thera. Copenhagen, Danish National Museum, Chr. VIII.324. Photo: Danish National Museum, Antiksamlingen

19 Bronze *fibula* from Crete. Athens, National Museum, 11765. Photo: German Archaeological Institute, Athens

20 Impression of stone seal. Paris, Bibliothèque Nationale, M 5837. Photo: M. Dudley

21 Bronze deer and fawn. Boston, Museum of Fine Arts, 98.650. Photo: courtesy Museum of Fine Arts

22 Bronze lion-hunt from Samos. Samos Museum. Photo: German Archaeological Institute, Athens

23 Bronze warrior from Karditsa. Athens, National Museum, 12831. Photo: Max Hirmer

24 Bronze tripod figure from Olympia. Olympia Museum, B 2800. Photo: German Archaeological Institute, Athens.

25 Clay figure from Thebes, Boeotia. Paris, Louvre, CA 623. Photo: Giraudon

26 Clay head from Amyclae. Athens, National Museum. Photo: German Archaeological Institute, Athens

27 Clay model shrine from Perachora. Athens, National Museum. After H. Payne, *Perachora* i pl. 9b

28 Clay model shrine from Arkhanes, Crete. Heraklion Museum. Photo: Max Hirmer

29 Gold ear-ring pendants. London, British Museum, 1960.11–1.18. Photo: courtesy the Trustees of the British Museum

30 Bronze griffin *protome* from Olympia. Olympia Museum, B 945. Photo: German Archaeological Institute, Athens

31 Ivory lion from Old Smyrna. Once Ankara University. Photo: courtesy J. M. Cook

32 Ivory youth from Samos. Samos Museum. Photo: German Archaeological Institute. Athens

33 Ivory group of two girls. New York. Metropolitan Museum of Art, 17.190.73. Gift of J. Pierpont Morgan, 1917. Photo: Metropolitan Museum of Art

34 Gold pendant from Khaniale Tekke, Knossos. Heraklion Museum. Photo: the author

35 Protocorinthian *oenochoe* from Cumae. Naples, National Museum

36 Protocorinthian *kotyle* from Camirus. London, British Museum, 60.4-4.18. Photo: courtesy the Trustees of the British Museum

37 Protocorinthian *aryballos* from Thebes. London, British Museum, 89.4-18.1. Photo: courtesy the Trustees of the British Museum

38 Detail from a Protocorinthian *olpe* ('Chigi vase') from near Veii. Rome, Villa Giulia. Photo: Max Hirmer

39 Fragment of a Protoattic plaque from Sunium. Athens, National Museum. Photo: German Archaeological Institute, Athens

40 Protoattic *amphora* from Attica. Berlin, Staatliche Museen, Antikenabteilung, 31006. Photo: Staatliche Museen

41 Detail of a Protoattic *amphora* from Eleusis. Eleusis Museum. Photo: German Archaeological Institute, Athens

42 Cycladic plate from Thasos. Thasos Museum. Photo: French School, Athens

43 Cycladic *oenochoe* from Aegina. London, British Museum, 73.8-20.385. Photo: courtesy the Trustees of the British Museum

44 Argive *crater* fragment from Argos. Argos Museum. Photo: French School, Athens

45 Detail of a 'Melian' *amphora* from Melos. Athens, National Museum, 3961. Photo: Max Hirmer

46 Rhodian *oenochoe*. Tübingen University Archaeological Institute, 1237. Photo: Archaeological Institute

47 Detail of a relief *amphora* from Mykonos. Mykonos Museum. Photo: German Archaeological Institute, Athens

48 Clay relief Gorgon from Syracuse. Syracuse, National Museum. Photo: Max Hirmer

49 Bronze plaque from Crete. Paris, Louvre, MNC 689. Photo: Giraudon

50 Bronze plaque from Olympia. Olympia Museum. After Kunze, *Meisterwerke der Kunst, Olympia*, fig. 34

51 Impression of white steatite seal. Oxford, Ashmolean Museum, 1921.1225. Photo: M. Dudley

52 Gold roundel. Paris, Bibliothèque Nationale. Photo: Bibliothèque Nationale

53 Bronze ram-bearer from Crete. Berlin, Staatliche Museen, Antikenabteilung, 7477. Photo: Staatliche Museen

54 Limestone statuette. Paris, Louvre, 3098. Photo: Max Hirmer

55 Marble *kouros* from Sunium. Athens, National Museum, 2720. Photo: Alison Frantz

56 Temple of Apollo, Corinth. Photo: Max Hirmer

57 Corner of Temple of Hera ('Basilica'), Paestum. Photo: Max Hirmer

58 Naxian sphinx on a column, from Delphi. Delphi Museum. Photo: Max Hirmer

59 Reconstruction by F. Krischen of the Temple of Artemis at Ephesus. Cf. Berve, Gruben, Hirmer, *Greek Temples, Theatres and Shrines* 459, fig. 126

60 Marble floral moulding from the Siphnian Treasury, Delphi. Photo: Max Hirmer

61 Marble *kouros* from Anavysos. Athens, National Museum, 3851. Photo: Max Hirmer

62 Marble rider from the Acropolis, Athens. Paris, Louvre, 3104 ('Rampin head'); Athens, Acropolis Museum, 590. Photo: Max Hirmer

63 Marble statue of a woman from Keratea. Berlin, Staatliche Museen, Antikenabteilung, 1800. Photo: Staatliche Museen

64 Marble *kore* from the Acropolis, Athens. Athens, Acropolis Museum, 679. Photo: Martin Hürlimann

65 Marble *kore* from the Acropolis, Athens. Athens, Acropolis Museum, 675. Photo: Max Hirmer

66 Marble *kore* from the Acropolis, Athens. Athens, Acropolis Museum, 670. Photo: Max Hirmer

67 Limestone metope from a building at Delphi. Delphi Museum. Photo: Max Hirmer

68 Limestone group from the Acropolis, Athens. Athens, Acropolis Museum. Photo: Max Hirmer

69 Marble warrior from the Temple of Aphaea, Aegina. Munich, Staatliche Antikensammlungen. Photo: Max Hirmer

70 Detail from the north frieze of the Siphnian Treasury, Delphi. Delphi Museum. Photo: Max Hirmer

71 Marble sphinx from Spata. Athens, National Museum, 28. Photo: Alison Frantz

72 Marble gravestone from Athens. Athens, National Museum, 29. Photo: Max Hirmer

73 Relief from a statue base, from the Kerameikos, Athens. Athens, National Museum, 3476. Photo: Max Hirmer

74 Marble relief from the Acropolis, Athens. Athens, Acropolis Museum, 1342. Photo: Max Hirmer

75 Detail of Athenian black-figure *skyphos-crater* from Vari. Athens, National Museum, 16383. Photo: TAP Service

76 Detail of Athenian black-figure volute *crater* ('François vase') from Chiusi. Florence, Museo Archeologico, 4209. Photo: Max Hirmer

77 Athenian black-figure plate. Munich, Staatliche Antikensammlungen, 8760. Photo: G. Wehrheim

78 Athenian black-figure *amphora*. Basel Antikenmuseum, Käppeli Collection. Photo: Antikenmuseum

79 Detail of Athenian black-figure *amphora* from Vulci. London, British Museum, B 210. Photo: Max Hirmer

80 Detail of Athenian black-figure band cup. Oxford, Oakeshott Collection. Photo: courtesy the Ashmolean Museum

81 Corinthian black-figure column *crater* from Cervetri. Rome, Vatican, Mus. Greg. Etr. 126. Photo: Max Hirmer

82 Corinthian black-figure plate from Corinth. Copenhagen, Danish National Museum, 1630. Photo: Danish National Museum, Antiksamlingen

83 Spartan black-figure cup from Italy. Paris, Louvre, E 668. Photo: Max Hirmer

84 East Greek cup from Etruria. Paris, Louvre, F 68. Photo: Max Hirmer

85 Chalcidian black-figure column *crater* from Vulci. Würzburg, Martin von Wagner Museum, 147. Photo: Martin von Wagner Museum

86 Caeretan black-figure *hydria* from Cervetri (Caere). Paris, Louvre, E 701. Photo: Max Hirmer

87 Detail of Athenian black-figure *amphora* from Vulci. Brescia, Museo Civico. Photo: Max Hirmer

88 Detail of Athenian red-figure *amphora* from Vulci. Berlin, Staatliche Museen, F 2159. Photo: Max Hirmer

89 Athenian red-figure cup from the Agora, Athens. Athens, Agora Museum, P 24102. Photo: Agora Excavations, American School of Classical Studies, Athens

90 Athenian red-figure *amphora* from Vulci. Munich, Staatliche Antikensammlungen, 2307. Photo: Max Hirmer

91 Athenian red-figure *amphora* from Etruria. Paris, Louvre, G 2. Photo: Max Hirmer

92 Clay plaque from the Acropolis, Athens. Athens, Acropolis Museum, 1037. Photo: German Archaeological Insitute, Athens

93 Detail of Athenian red-figure *amphora* from Vulci. Berlin, Staatliche Museen, Antikenabteilung, F 2160. Photo: Max Hirmer

94 Athenian red-figure cup from Orvieto. Boston, Museum of Fine Arts, 10.179. Photo: courtesy Museum of Fine Arts

95 Detail of Athenian red-figure *amphora* from Vulci. Munich, Staatliche Antikensammlungen, 2344. Photo: Max Hirmer

96 Athenian red-figure *psykter* from Cervetri. London, British Museum, E 768. Photo: courtesy the Trustees of the British Museum

97 Detail of Athenian red-figure cup. Paris, Louvre, G 156. Photo: Max Hirmer

98 Wall painting from Gordion, Phrygia. Photo: Pennsylvania University Museum

99 Clay figure vase from the Agora, Athens. Athens, Agora Museum, P 1231. Photo: Agora Excavations, American School of Classical Studies, Athens

100 Clay head of a silen from Gela. Gela Antiquario. Photo: Max Hirmer

101 Bronze figurine of a symposiast from Dodona. London, British Museum, 1954.10–18.1. Photo: Max Hirmer

102 Bronze vase from Paestum. Paestum Museum. Photo: H. Wagner, Heidelberg

103 Bronze mirror support. New York, Metropolitan Museum of Art, Fletcher Fund, 1938.11.3. Photo: Metropolitan Museum of Art

104 Impression of agate scarab. London, British Museum, Walters 465. Photo: M. L. Vollenweider

105 Silver coin of Athens. London, British Museum. Photo: courtesy the Trustees of the British Museum

106 Marble youth from the Acropolis, Athens. Athens, Acropolis Museum, 698. Photo: Max Hirmer

107 Restored drawing of the east end of the Temple of Zeus at Olympia. Cf. Berve, Gruben, Hirmer, *Greek Temples, Theatres and Shrines* 320, fig. 9

108 Metope from the Temple of Zeus at Olympia. Olympia Museum. Photo: Max Hirmer

109 Head of a centaur from the west pediment of the Temple of Zeus at Olympia. Olympia Museum. Photo: the author

110 Detail of Apollo from the west pediment of the Temple of Zeus at Olympia. Olympia Museum. Photo: Max Hirmer

111 Clay group of Zeus and Ganymede from Olympia. Olympia Museum. Photo: Max Hirmer

112 Detail of bronze statue from the Artemisium wreck. Athens, National Museum, 15161. Photo: Max Hirmer

113 Bronze head from Salamis, Cyprus. London, British Museum. Photo: courtesy the Trustees of the British Museum

114 Marble relief from the Acropolis, Athens. Athens, Acropolis Museum, 1707. Photo: Max Hirmer

115 Marble gravestone, probably from Paros. Berlin, Staatliche Museen, Antikenabteilung, 1482. Photo: Staatliche Museen

116 Model of the Acropolis, Athens. Royal Ontario Museum, University of Toronto. Photo: Royal Ontario Museum

117 The Parthenon on the Acropolis, Athens. Photo: Max Hirmer

118 Group of three goddesses from the east pediment of the Parthenon. London, British Museum. Photo: Max Hirmer

119 The Propylaea to the Acropolis, Athens. Photo: Max Hirmer

120 Metope from the Parthenon. London, British Museum. Photo: Max Hirmer

121 Detail from the Parthenon frieze. London, British Museum. Photo: Max Hirmer

122 North porch of the Erechtheion on the Acropolis, Athens. Photo: Max Hirmer

123 Caryatid from the Erechtheion on the Acropolis, Athens. London, British Museum. Photo: Max Hirmer

124 West end of the Temple of Hephaistos, Athens. Photo: the author

125 Relief from the balustrade of the Temple of Athena Nike on the Acropolis, Athens. Athens, Acropolis Museum. Photo: Max Hirmer

126 Temple of Apollo Epikourios at Bassae. Photo: Max Hirmer

127 Restored drawing by F. Krischen of the interior of the Temple of Apollo at Bassae. Cf. Berve, Gruben, Hirmer, *Greek Temples, Theatres and Shrines* 353, fig. 43

128 Slab from the frieze of the Temple of Apollo, Bassae. London, British Museum. Photo: courtesy the Trustees of the British Museum

129 Marble statue of a woman from Persepolis. Teheran Museum. Photo: courtesy Erich F. Schmidt, Oriental Institute, University of Chicago

130 Marble relief from Phaleron. Athens, National Museum, 1783. Photo: German Archaeological Institute, Athens

131 Marble statue of a Niobid from Rome. Rome, Terme Museum, 72274. Photo: Max Hirmer

132 The lion of Chaeronea. Photo: Max Hirmer

133 Marble head from Melos. London, British Museum, 550. Photo: Max Hirmer

134 Figure from the 'Nereid Monument', Xanthos. London, British Museum. Photo: Max Hirmer

135 Bronze youth from the Marathon wreck. Athens, National Museum, 15118. Photo: Max Hirmer

136 Marble statue of Hermes from Olympia. Olympia Museum. Photo: Max Hirmer

137 Marble statue of Demeter from Cnidus. London, British Museum, 1300. Photo: Max Hirmer

138 Marble gravestone of Theano from Athens. Athens, National Museum, 3472. Photo: Max Hirmer

139 Marble statue from the Mausoleum, Halicarnassus. London, British Museum, 1000. Photo: Max Hirmer

140 Restored drawing of the theatre at Priene. Cf. Berve, Gruben, Hirmer, *Greek Temples, Theatres and Shrines* 474, fig. 138

141 Carved entablature from the Tholos, Epidaurus. Photo: Max Hirmer

142 Tholos, on Marmaria, Delphi. Photo: Max Hirmer

143 Marble relief from Rome. Rome, Terme Museum, 8670. Photo: Max Hirmer

144 Copy of the Doryphorus of Polyclitus. Naples, National Museum. Photo: Anderson

145 Copy of the Aphrodite of Cnidus by Praxiteles. Rome, Vatican Museums. Photo: Archivio fotografico dei Gallerie e Musei Vaticani

146 Copy of the Apoxyomenus by Lysippus. Rome, Vatican Museums. Photo: Archivio fotografico dei Gallerie e Musei Vaticani

147 Clay figure of a dancer from Locri. Reggio, National Museum, 4823. Photo: Max Hirmer

148 Clay plaque from Locri. Taranto, National Museum, IG 8326. Photo: Max Hirmer

149 Clay group of actors. Würzburg, Martin von Wagner Museum. Photo: Martin von Wagner Museum

150 Clay figure vase from Capua. Boston, Museum of Fine Arts, 98.881. Photo: courtesy Museum of Fine Arts

151 Clay relief *rhyton*. Oxford, Ashmolean Museum, 1947.374. Photo: courtesy the Ashmolean Museum

152 Bronze mirror-cover from Elis. Athens, National Museum, Stathatou Collection. Photo: courtesy of Mme Stathatou

153 Gilt bronze mirror-cover. Paris, Louvre, MND 262. Photo: Giraudon

154 Detail of bronze satyr on a relief vase from Derveni. Salonika Museum. Photo: courtesy of Professor Makaronas

155 Bronze mirror-support. Dublin, National Museum of Ireland. Photo: National Museum of Ireland

156 Bronze runner. Tübingen, University Archaeological Institute. Photo: Archaeological Institute

157 Bronze Pan from Lousoi. Berlin, Staatliche Museen, Antikenabteilung, 8624. Photo: Staatliche Museen

158 Bronze girl from Verroia. Munich, Staatliche Antikensammlungen, 3669. Photo: Staatliche Antikensammlungen

159 Gold *phiale* from Kul Oba. Leningrad, Hermitage Museum. Photo: Hermitage Museum

160 Gold ear-rings from Tarentum. Taranto, National Museum, 54115. Photo: Soprintendenza alle Antichità, Taranto

161 Gold diadem from near Tarentum. Taranto, National Museum, 54114. Photo: Max Hirmer

162 Chalcedony scaraboid, from Kerch, South Russia. Leningrad, Hermitage Museum. Photo: M. L. Vollenweider

163 Silver coins of Syracuse and Clazomenae. Paris, Bibliothèque Nationale. Photo: Bibliothèque Nationale

164 Ivory plaques from Kul Oba. Leningrad, Hermitage Museum. Photo: Hermitage Museum

165 Gravestone of Mnason from Thebes. Thebes Museum. Photo: German Archaeological Institute, Athens

166 Pebble mosaic from a house at Olynthus. Photo: University of Mississippi

167 Athenian red-figure *lekythos* from Gela. Boston, Museum of Fine Arts, 13.198. Photo: courtesy Museum of Fine Arts

168 Detail of Athenian red-figure volute *crater* from Gela. Palermo, National Museum, G 1283. Photo: Max Hirmer

169 Athenian red-figure calyx *crater* from Orvieto. Paris, Louvre, MNC 511. Photo: Max Hirmer

170 Detail of Athenian red-figure *stamnos*. Cape Town, South African Museum. Photo: South African Museum

171 Athenian red-figure *skyphos* from Cervetri. Schwerin Museum, 708. Photo: Max Hirmer

172 Athenian white-ground cup from Camirus. London, British Museum, D 2. Photo: courtesy the Trustees of the British Museum

173 Detail of Athenian white-ground *lekythos* from Eretria. Athens, National Museum, 1818. Photo: Martin Hürlimann

174 Detail of Athenian white-ground *lekythos* from Attica. Lugano, von Schoen Collection. Photo: Max Hirmer

175 Detail of Athenian red-figure *stamnos* from Vulci. Munich, Staatliche Antikensammlungen, 2415. Photo: Max Hirmer

176 Athenian white-ground *lekythos* from Eretria. Athens, National Museum, 1816. Photo: Max Hirmer

177 Athenian red-figure squat *lekythos*. New York, Metropolitan Museum of Art, Fletcher Fund, 1930.11.8. Photo: Metropolitan Museum of Art

178 Detail of Athenian red-figure *amphora* from Vulci. Rome, Vatican Museums. Photo: Max Hirmer

179 Athenian red-figure *pelike* from Camirus. London, British Museum, E 424. Photo: Max Hirmer

180 Detail of Athenian red-figure *hydria* from Ruvo. Karlsruhe, Badisches Landesmuseum, 259. Photo: Badisches Landesmuseum

181 Detail of South Italian red-figure volute *crater* from Ceglie del Campo. Taranto, National Museum, 8263. Photo: Max Hirmer

182 South Italian red-figure squat *lekythos* from Tarentum. Taranto, National Museum, 4530. Photo: Max Hirmer

183 Apulian red-figure bell *crater*. London, Victoria and Albert Museum, 1776–1919

184 Boeotian Cabirion *skyphos*. New York, Sonnenberg Collection

185 Boeotian floral *pyxis*. Reading University Museum, 26.iv.1. Photo: Reading Museum

186 Double convex quartz gem. Oxford, Ashmolean Museum, Department of Antiquities 1892.1199. Photo: M. L. Vollenweider

187 Copy of the Tyche of Antioch. Rome, Vatican Museums. Photo: Archivio fotografico dei Gallerie e Musei Vaticani

188 Restored model of the Acropolis at Pergamum. Berlin, Staatliche Museen, Antikenabteilung. Photo: Staatliche Museen

189 Temple of Artemis at Sardis. Photo: Max Hirmer

190 Restored model of the Stoa of Attalus in the Agora, Athens. Athens, Agora Museum. Photo: Agora Excavations, American School of Classical Studies, Athens

191 Tower at Perge. Photo: Courtauld Institute of Art, London

192 Great Altar at Pergamum. Berlin, Staatliche Museen, Antikenabteilung. Photo: Max Hirmer

193 Detail of the Great Altar at Pergamum. Berlin. Photo: Staatliche Museen

194 Copy of the group of a Gaul and his wife. Rome, Terme Museum. Photo: Max Hirmer

195 Marble group of Laocoön and his sons. Rome, Vatican Museums. Photo: Archivio fotografico dei Gallerie e Musei Vaticani

196 Marble statue of a man and woman on Delos. Photo: Max Hirmer

197 The Victory from Samothrace. Paris, Louvre. Photo: Max Hirmer

198 Marble statue of a boy from Tralles. Istanbul Museum. Photo: Max Hirmer

199 Copy of the crouching Aphrodite by Doidalsas. Paris, Louvre. Photo: Alinari

200 Statue of Aphrodite from Melos. Paris, Louvre. Photo: Max Hirmer

201 Copy of sleeping hermaphrodite. Rome, Terme Museum. Photo: Anderson

202 Marble sleeping satyr. Munich, Staatliche Antikensammlungen, 218. Photo: Max Hirmer

203 Bronze boxer. Rome, Terme Museum, 1055. Photo: Max Hirmer

204 Copy of a portrait of Epicurus. New York, Metropolitan Museum of Art, Rogers Fund, 1911.90. Photo: Metropolitan Museum of Art

205 Copy of a statue of Demosthenes. Rome, Vatican Museums. Photo: German Archaeological Institute, Rome

206 Bronze statue of a prince. Rome, Terme Museum, 1049. Photo: Max Hirmer

207 Bronze head from Delos. Athens, National Museum, 14612. Photo: Max Hirmer

208 Marble relief. London, British Museum, 2191. Photo: courtesy the Trustees of the British Museum

209 Marble relief from near Corinth. Munich, Staatliche Antikensammlungen, 206. Photo: Kaufmann

210 Detail from the 'Alexander sarcophagus' from Sidon. Istanbul. Photo: Max Hirmer

211 Marble *lutrophoros* from Athens. Athens, National Museum. Photo: Alinari

212 Clay group from Capua. London, British Museum, D 161. Photo: Max Hirmer

213 Clay head from Tarentum. Taranto, National Museum, 20068. Photo: Max Hirmer

214 Clay figure from Tanagra. Berlin, Staatliche Museen, Antikenabteilung, TC 7674. Photo: Staatliche Museen

215 Clay figure from Tarentum. Taranto, National Museum, 52074. Photo: Max Hirmer

216 Bronze figure of a Negro boy. Paris, Bibliothèque Nationale, 1009. Photo: Giraudon

217 Clay figure vase. Würzburg, Martin von Wagner Museum, 4958. Photo: Martin von Wagner Museum

218 Bronze statuette of a philosopher. New York, Metropolitan Museum of Art, Rogers Fund, 1910.231.1. Photo: Metropolitan Museum of Art

219 Bronze statuette of a god. Paris, Louvre, MND 2014. Photo: Archives Photographiques

220 Gold *amphora* from Panagurishte. Archaeological Museum, Plowdiw, Bulgaria. Photo: Dr Helga Reusch

221 Gold and silver *pyxis* lid from near Tarentum. Taranto, National Museum, 22429. Photo: Max Hirmer

222 Gold diadem from Thessaly. Athens, Benaki Museum. Photo: Benaki Museum

223 Gold ears of wheat from near Syracuse. Collection: Mr and Mrs J. W. Hambuechen, USA

224 Clay *hydria* from Arsinoe. Brussels, A 13. Photo: A. C. L., Brussels

225 *Kantharos* from Vulci. Collection: Prinz Philipp von Hessen. Photo: R. and R. Büttner, Fulda

226 Plate from Capena. Rome, Villa Giulia Museum, 23949. Photo: Alinari

227 Gnathia *crater*. Leiden, Rijksmuseum van Oudheden, B 677. Photo: Rijksmuseum van Oudheden

228 Clay *hydria* from Naples. Copenhagen, Danish National Museum, Antiksamlingen, 3240. Photo: Danish National Museum, Antiksamlingen

229 Clay relief bowl. London, British Museum, 1902.12-18.4. Photo: courtesy the Trustees of the British Museum

230 Impression of beryl gem stone. Boston, Museum of Fine Arts (Lewes House 94)

231 Silver coins of Antiochus I and Arsinoe III. Paris, Bibliothèque Nationale. Photo: Bibliothèque Nationale

232 *Crater* from Centuripe. Catania University. Photo: Max Hirmer

233 Painted tombstone from Pagasai. Volos Museum. Photo: Alison Frantz

234 Blue marble tombstone of Metrodorus from Chios. Berlin, Staatliche Museen, Antikenabteilung, 766A. Photo: Staatliche Museen

235 Detail of the 'Alexander mosaic' from Pompeii. Naples, National Museum. Photo: André Held

236 Stag-hunt mosaic at Pella

237 Detail of an Etruscan black-figure vase. Munich, Staatliche Antikensammlungen, 838. Photo: Martin Hürlimann

238 Painting from the Tomba dei Tori, Tarquinia

239 Painting from the Tomba del Orco, Tarquinia

240 Etruscan red-figure *skyphos*. Boston, Museum of Fine Arts, 97.372. Photo: courtesy Museum of Fine Arts

241 Marble relief from the Piraeus. Piraeus Museum. Photo: Max Hirmer

242 Marble relief. Copenhagen, Ny Carlsberg Glyptotek, 30. Photo: Ny Carlsberg Glyptotek

243 Wooden portrait panel, from the Fayum, Egypt. New York, Metropolitan Museum of Art, Rogers Fund, 09.181.1. Photo: Metropolitan Museum of Art

244 Marble group of a youth and a woman. Naples, National Museum. Photo: Anderson

245 Marble head of a priest from the Agora, Athens. Athens, Agora Museum, S 333. Photo: Agora Excavations, American School of Classical Studies, Athens

246 'Perseus and Andromeda', painting from Pompeii. Naples, National Museum. Photo: André Held

247 'Heracles and Telephos', painting from Herculaneum. Naples, National Museum. Photo: André Held

248 'The Three Graces', painting from Pompeii. Naples, National Museum. Photo: André Held

249 'The Three Graces', by Raphael. Musée Condé, Chantilly. Photo: Archives Photographiques

250 Arretine mould for a vase. New York, Metropolitan Museum of Art, Rogers Fund, 1919.192.24. Photo: Metropolitan Museum of Art

251 *Stoa* at Camirus. Photo: the author

The author and publishers are grateful to the many official bodies, institutions and individuals mentioned above for their assistance in supplying original illustration material.

281

All numbers refer to text pages; those in italic indicate illustrations

Achilles Painter: *lekythoi*, 188, 189, 191; name-vase, detail, 194

Aegina: griffin jug, 54, 55; sculptures from Temple of Aphaea, 13, 84

Aeolic capitals, 70

Alcaeus, 267

Alcamenes, 158

Alexander III, the Great, 144, 145, 203, 204, 224

'Alexander sarcophagus', 229, 230

Alexandria, 204, 241; *Pharos*, 209

Al Mina, 41

Altamura Painter, 184

Amasis Painter, 92, 102; *amphora*, 93

Amyclae, clay head from temple, 37

Anavysos, *kouros*, 74

Andocides Painter, 104; vase, 103

Antioch, 204; city-goddess, 205

Apelles, 250

Apollonius of Athens, 223; boxer, detail, 223

Apollonius of Rhodes, 228

Apoxyomenus of Lysippus, copy, 160

Apulia, *lekythos*, 199

Archaic reliefs, copies, 258, 260

Archer, A., painting of Elgin Room, 13

architecture: Archaic, 69–73; Classical, 150–3; Eighth-century, 38–40; Hellenistic, 206–10; monumental stone, 60; Roman, influenced by Greek, 266; temple, 72–3

Argos, 33, 55; vase fragment, 55

Aristocles, 86

Arles, Venus of, 12

Arsinoe, *hydria*, 241

Artemisium, bronze figure from wreck, 125

Arundel, second Earl of, 12–13

Ashmolean Museum, Oxford, staircase, 14

Athanodoros, 214

Athens, 127–38; Acropolis, 9, 22, 128–35, 206, 208; Athena Promachos, 129; clay plaque, 106; Erechtheion, 9, 134–8, 267; Caryatid from south porch, 135; north porch, 134; *korai*, 79, 81; limestone group, 83; marble votive relief, 88; Parthenon, 129–35; frieze, detail, 133; pediment, group of goddesses, 130; 'peplos kore', 78, 80; Propylaea, 131; 'Rampin horseman', 75, 76; Temple of Athena Nike, 137–8; balustrade, 136; votive relief of Athena, 127; Altar of the Twelve Gods, 258; relief, 15, 17; cemetery, funeral vase, 232; Hephaisteion, 136, 138; statue base relief, 87; Stoa of Attalus, model, 209; Tower of the Winds, 209

Attalus I, dedication at Pergamum, 213

'Auxerre goddess', 65

Barberini faun, 222

Bassae, Temple of Apollo, 139–40; frieze, 140; cast, 14; interior, 139

'Berlin goddess', 77

Berlin Painter, 106; name-vase, detail, 107

Bernini, L., 222

black-figure technique: Corinthian, 48; Athenian, 89

Boeotia, 33; Cabirion cup, 201; clay figure, 36, 37; *pyxis*, 202

Brauron, sanctuary, 17

British Museum, Temporary Elgin Room, 13

bronze: casting technique, 172; Classical Greek, 167–73; figurines; armed runner, 171; Geometric, 34, 35, 36; Hellenistic, 237; man reclining, 114; Pan, from Arcadia, 172; Seventh-century statuette, 63; Verroia, naked

girl, *173*; griffin cauldron attachments, 42, *43*; mirror, *116*, *167*; cover, *168*; support, *170*; plaques, *60*, *61*; vase from Paestum, *115*
Brygos Painter, 110; cup,. *111*

Cabirion, 201
Caere, 98
Callicrates, 129
cameos, 245–6
Camirus, reinforced concrete colonnade, *267*
Canova, 9
Capua, clay group, *233*
Carlsruhe Paris Painter, vase detail, *196*
Carthage, 153
caryatids, 9, 73, 84
Chaeronea, Lion of, *144*
'Chatsworth head', *126*
Chicago Painter, 186; vase, *185*
'Chigi vase', detail, *50*
Chios: gilt bronze horse at Venice, *11*; gravestone of Metrodorus, *249*
clay figurines: Geometric, *36*, *37*; Archaic, 113–14; Classical Greek, 161–6; Hellenistic, 233–5
clay relief work, 57–60
Clazomenae, coin, *177*
Cnidus, 207; Aphrodite, 146; copy, *159*; Demeter and Kore Sanctuary, seated figure, *148*
Cockerell, C. R., 14
Coins, Athenian, *117*; Antiochus I, *246*; Arsinoe III, *246*; Classical Greek, 177–8; Clazomenae, *177*; electrum, 116–17; Hellenistic, 245–6; Philip II, *169*; Syracuse, *177*
Constantinople, Hippodrome, 11
Corinth, 47–8, 51, 89, 91, 253; Temple of Apollo, *67*
costume: Archaic, 77, 79–80; Athenian, 182; Classical, 127–8; stage, 163, *164*
Cresilas, 158
Crete, 21; bronze plaque, *60*; clay head, 24, *25*
'Critian boy', *118*
Cumae, Protocorinthian jug, *47*

Dedalic style, 64
Delos, 66; bronze portrait head, *227*; marble lion at Venice, *10*, 12
Delphi, 17; charioteer, 126; Naxian sphinx, *70*, 72; Sicyonian building metope, *82*; Siphnian Treasury frieze, *72*, 84, *85*; Tholos, 152, *154*
Demetrius of Phaleron, 229
Demetrius I of Syria, portrait, *226*
Demosthenes, portrait, *225*
Derveni, tomb, reclining satyr, detail, *169*
Dexamenos of Chios, 176; engraved gem, *176*
Doidalsas, 218; crouching Aphrodite, copy, *218*
Donatello, 11
Doric order, 69, 266
Doryphorus of Polyclitus, copy, *157*
Douris, 110

Egyptian influence, 21, 41–65, 69
Eleusis, Protoattic grave vase, *52*
Elgin Marbles, 9, 13–14, 130–33
encaustic technique, 259
Ephesus, Temple of Artemis, 83–4; restoration, *71*
Epicurus, portrait, *224*, 237
Epidaurus, Tholos, 152; carved entablature, *153*
Epiktetos, 107; *see also* Kleophrades Painter
Eretria Painter, *lekythos*, *193*
Ergotimos, 91
Etruria, 14, 112, 242, 252–7
Euboea, 202
Eumenes II, 211
Euphronios, 105
Euthymides, 105, 106, 112
Evans, Sir A., 21
Exekias, 92, 95, 105

fibulae, 34; Boeotian type, *33*
figure treatment: Archaic, 73–81; Classical, 122–6; Fourth-century, 146–9; Geometric, 28–9; Hellenistic, 218

Finlay, G., 14
'François vase', 91

Gela, clay antefix, *113*
gem engraving, 115–17, 245; beryl gem
    impression, *245*; Dexamenos of Chios,
    gem, *176*; head of Alexander, *204*;
    'Island Gems', 61, 62
Geometric art, 21, 25–9, 33–7

Hagesandros, 214
Halicarnassus, Mausoleum, 150, 151
Harmodius, 118
Herculaneum, 262; wall painting, *263*
Hermaphrodite figures, 218, *220*
'Hesse group', 242
Homer, 30
Hunt Painter, name-piece, *97*

Iktinos, 129, 139
Italy, South, 153; Greek clay cup, *166*
ivory carving, 41; boy from Samos, *45*;
    Geometric group of maidens, *42*;
    girls, *45*; lion, *44*; plaques, Kul Oba
    tomb, 178, *179*; seals, *44*

jewellery, 40; diadem, gold, *240*; ear-
    rings, gold, *40*; from Tarentum, *175*;
    funeral wreaths, 240, *241*; pendant,
    46; rings, 175–6, 245
Jones, Inigo, 12

Karditsa, bronze warrior, *35*
Karneia Painter, vase detail, *197*
Keratea, 'Berlin goddess', *77*
Kleitias, 91
Kleophon Painter, vase detail, *190*
Kleophrades Painter (Epiktetos), 106–8;
    vase detail, *109*
Knossos, gold pendant, *46*
korai, 76, *78*, *79*, *81*
kouroi, *16*, 65, *66*, 73, 76
Krischen, F., 71
Kul Oba, tomb; gold *phiale*, *174*; ivory
    plaques, 178, *179*

Laocoön group, *214*
Leochares, 148
Locri, 164; clay figure of maenad, *162*;
    clay plaque, *163*
Louis XIV, 12
'Ludovisi throne', *155*
Lydos, Athenian plate, *92*
Lysippus, 158, 203, 215, 224, 225;
    Apoxyomenus, copy, *160*

'Macmillan *aryballos*', *49*
Marathon, bronze statue from wreck,
    147
Marsyas Painter, *pelike*, *195*
Mausolus, 150, *151*
Megacles, 106
Meidias Painter, 196
Melos: clay plaques, 164; marble
    head, *145*; Venus, 218, *219*
Michelangelo, 10
Mikon, 178
Mnesicles, 131
mosaic: Classical Greek, 178–80;
    Hellenistic, 250–2; Olynthus, pebble
    mosaic, *181*; Pella, pebble mosaic,
    251
mummy-case portrait, *259*
Mycenae, 21; Lion Gate, 22, *23*
Mykonos, clay relief vase neck, *58*
Myron, 159
Mytens, 12
mythical scenes on vases, 30

Napoleon, 12
Negroes, treatment in Greek sculpture,
    234, *236*
Neo-Attic reliefs, 260
'Nereid Monument', nymph from,
    146
Nessos Painter, 89, 91; vase, *90*
Nikias, 262
Niobid Painter, 183, 184, 185, 186;
    name-vase, *184*; vase, *183*
Niobids group, 142, *143*, 257

Oltos, 106; vase, *105*
Olympia, 120–6, 130, 131; clay group, *124*; cup from Phidias's studio, *19*; figure from bronze cauldron, *36*; Temple of Hera, Hermes, 148; Temple of Zeus, *119*, 120–23; Apollo, detail, *123*; Head of centaur, *121*; Metope, *120*
Olynthus, pebble mosaic, *181*
Onesimos, 108–10
Ostia, 210

Paestum: bronze vase detail, *115*; Temple of Hera, *68*
Pagasai-Demetrias, tombstone detail, *248*
painting: Classical Greek technique, 178; encaustic technique, 259; Hellenistic, 246–51
Panagurishte hoard, 17, 239; *amphora*, *238*
Pan Painter, 183; *lekythos*, *182*
Paris, 12
Parrhasios, 261
Parthenon sculptures *see* Athens
Pasiteles, 260
Pella, pebble mosaic, *251*
Penrose, 'Athenian', 14
Penthesilea Painter, 186
'*Peplos kore*', *78*, 80
Perachora: clay model, *38*; *phialae* from lake, 174
Pergamum, 204, 206–8; Acropolis, model, *206*; dedication by Attalus, *213*; Great Altar of Zeus, 13, 208, 211–14; frieze detail, *212*; north wing, *211*
Perge, tower, *210*
Pericles, 128
Persepolis, mourning woman statue, *141*
Persia, 118, 119, 128
Petrarch, 11
phialae: Kul Oba, *174*; Perachora, 174
Phidias, 18, 122, 129, 132, 158, 257; inscribed mug, 18, *19*
Philip of Macedon, 144; coin, *169*

phlyax vases, 198, *200*
Phradmon, 158
Phrygia, 112
Piraeus, 17; head of bronze *kouros*, *16*; marble reliefs from wreck, *257*, *258*
Piranesi, G. B., 10
Pistoxenos Painter, 186; cup, *186*; white-ground cup, *187*
Pliny, 203
Polyclitus, 157, 159
Polydoros, 214
Polyeuktos, 225
Polygnotus, 178
Pompeii: Alexander mosaic, 250; detail, *250*; House of Dioscurides, painting, *262*; wall paintings, 262–4
portraiture: Greek, 150; Hellenistic, 224–7; Roman, 261
pottery: *amphorae*, *2*, *24*, *31*, *32*, *93*, *94*, *101*, *105*, *107*; Argive, *55*; Arretine ware, 264; mould, *266*; *aryballoi*, 48, 49; black-figure, 48, 89, 91; Boeotian, *202*; Cabirion, *201*; Caeretan, *100*; Chalcidian, 97, *99*; Corinthian, 93, *95*, *96*; *craters*, *26*, *28*, *29*, *91*, *95*, *99*; cups, *19*, *48*, *94*, *97*, *104*, *108*, *111*, *166*, *187*, *201*, *242*, *256*; Etruscan, *252*, *256*; funerary vase, *247*; Geometric, *2*, *25–34*, *26*, *28*, *29*; Gnathia, *243*; grave vases, *90*; Hadra, 240, 241; 'Hesse group', *242*; *hydriae*, 98, *100*, 241, *244*; jugs, *47*, *54*; *kantharoi*, *30*; *kylikes*, 108; Late Geometric, *30*, *31*, *32*; *lekythoi*, *182*, *188*, *189*, *192*, *193*, *199*; Megarian, 243–5; 'Melian', 56; Panathenaic *amphorae*, 102; *pelike*, *195*; *phlyax* vases, 198, *200*; plates, *53*, *92*, *96*, *242*; polychrome, 246, *247*; Protoattic, *50*, *51*, *52*, *53*; Protocorinthian, *47*, *48*, *49*, *50*; Protogeometric, *24*; *psykter*, *110*; *pyxis*, *202*; red-figure, 95, 102–12, 198; relief decorated, 57–9, *244*; Samian, 264; *skyphos*, *186*; Spartan, 96, *97*; West Slope ware, 243; 'wild goat style', *56*, *57*; *see also* individual vases and painters, also vase painting

285

Praxiteles, 12, 146, 148; Cnidian Aphrodite, copy, *159*, 218
Priene, theatre, reconstruction, *152*
Protogeometric art, 24–5
Psiax, 101

Raphael, 'The Three Graces', *265*
red-figure technique: Athenian, 95, 102–12; South Italian, 198
Rhegium, 97
Rhodes, Colossus, 216
Romans, 253–67
Rubens, P. P., 12

St Pancras Church, 9
Samos, 98; bronze group from, *35*; Heraion, 17
Samothrace, Victory, *216*
Sappho, 268
Sardis, Temple of Artemis, *207*
Schliemann, H., 9, 21
Scopas, 158
sculpture: Archaic, 73–89; Classical and Classical fourth-century copies, 156–60; early Greek, 62–6; Hellenistic, 211–36; groups, 222
seals, 34; 'Island Gems', *62*; ivory, 61; Late Geometric stone, *34*
Seleucia, 206
Sicily, Greeks in, 153
Sidon, 'Alexander sarcophagus', *230*
Smyrna, 206; figurines, 234; ivory lion from Old Smyrna, *44*
Socrates, 225, 261
Sophilos, 102
Sotades Painter, *165*
Sparta, 117; clay head, *37*; pottery, 96, 97
Spata, sphinx from gravestone, *86*
stage, Athenian costume, 163, *164*
Sulla, 17
Sunium: marble *kouros*, *65*; Protoattic clay plaque, *50*
Syracuse: coin, *177*; Temple of Athena, 267

Tanagra figurines, 233, *235*
Tarentum, 164; clay figure of woman, *235*; gold diadem, *176*; gold ear-rings, *175*; grotesque clay mask, *234*; silver box lid, *239*
Tarquinia: Tomba del Orca, head of Velia, *255*; Tomba dei Tori, painting, *254*
Terme boxer, 222; detail, *223*
terracottas *see* clay figurines
Thasos, plate, *53*
Thebes: Cabirion cup, *201*; gravestone of Mnason, *180*
Theodorus of Phocaea, 154
Thera, Late Geometric vase, *32*
Theseion *see* Athens, Hephaisteion
Thessaly, gold diadem, *240*
Three Maidens Painter, *crater*, *95*
Thurii, vase painters, 198
Tivoli, Hadrian's Villa, 10
Trajan, 208
Tralles, boy, sculpture, 216, *217*
Tyche, *205*

Vari, grave vase, detail, *90*
vase painting: Archaic, 89–112; Classical, 180–202; technique, 187–91; Geometric, 47–56; Hellenistic, 240–5; Polychrome, 240–2
Vatican, copy of Praxiteles's Aphrodite, 12, *159*, 218
Venice: gilt bronze horses, *11*, 12; marble lions, *10*, 12
Venus de Milo, 218, *219*
Verroia, bronze figure of girl, *173*
Villa Giulia Painter, 186
Vix, 17; *crater*, *115*
votive reliefs, Hellenistic, *228*, *229*
Vulci, cup, *242*

Wedgwood, J., 243
wood sculpture, 63

Xanthos, nymph from 'Nereid Monument', *146*
Xenophon, 261

The World of Art Library

History of Art

THE ART OF THE ANCIENT NEAR EAST *Seton Lloyd*
GREEK ART *John Boardman*
ROMAN ART AND ARCHITECTURE *Sir Mortimer Wheeler*
ART OF THE EARLY CHRISTIANS *Michael Gough*
ART OF THE BYZANTINE ERA *David Talbot Rice*
EARLY MEDIEVAL ART *John Beckwith*
ART OF CHINA, KOREA AND JAPAN *Peter Swann*
ISLAMIC ART *David Talbot Rice*
THE ART OF THE RENAISSANCE *P. & L. Murray*
LATE RENAISSANCE AND MANNERISM *P. & L. Murray*
BAROQUE AND ROCOCO *Germain Bazin*
ART OF THE ROMANTIC ERA *Marcel Brion*
IMPRESSIONISM *Phoebe Pool*
PREHISTORIC ART *T. G. E. Powell*
ART OF LATIN AMERICA *G. H. S. Bushnell*
THE ARTS OF CENTRAL ASIA *Tamara Talbot Rice*
A CONCISE HISTORY OF ENGLISH PAINTING *William Gaunt*
A CONCISE HISTORY OF RUSSIAN ART *Tamara Talbot Rice*
A CONCISE HISTORY OF MODERN PAINTING *Sir Herbert Read*
EUROPEAN SCULPTURE *H. D. Molesworth*
A CONCISE HISTORY OF MODERN SCULPTURE *Sir Herbert Read*

Artists

CHAGALL *Jean Cassou*
DÜRER *Marcel Brion*
GAUGUIN *Georges Boudaille*
VAN GOGH *Pierre Cabanne*
GOYA *J.-F. Chabrun*
KLEE *G. di San Lazzaro*
MICHELANGELO *Rolf Schott*
PICASSO *Pierre Daix*
RENOIR *François Fosca*
SEURAT *John Russell*
TOULOUSE-LAUTREC *Jean Bouret*

Galleries

THE NATIONAL GALLERY LONDON   *Sir Philip Hendy*
THE TATE GALLERY   *Sir John Rothenstein*
THE LOUVRE   *Germain Bazin*
IMPRESSIONIST PAINTINGS IN THE LOUVRE   *Germain Bazin*
THE SCHOOL OF PARIS (MUSÉE D'ART MODERNE)   *Bernard Dorival*
THE PRADO   *Sanchez Canton*
DUTCH MUSEUMS   *R. Van Luttervelt*
THE DRESDEN GALLERY   *Henner Menz*
THE HERMITAGE   *Pierre Descargues*
THE NATIONAL GALLERY WASHINGTON   *John Walker*
THE UFFIZI AND PITTI   *Filippo Rossi*

General

A CONCISE HISTORY OF ART (2 vols.)   *Germain Bazin*
THE ARTS OF MAN   *Eric Newton*
ENCYCLOPAEDIA OF OLD MASTERS   *Joachim Fernau*
A CONCISE HISTORY OF PAINTING:
FROM GIOTTO TO CÉZANNE   *Michael Levey*
THE WORLD OF THE IMPRESSIONISTS   *François Mathey*
PRIMITIVE ART   *Douglas Fraser*
MASTERS OF THE JAPANESE PRINT   *Richard Lane*
GRAPHIC ART OF THE 18TH CENTURY   *Jean Adhémar*
GRAPHIC ART OF THE 19TH CENTURY   *Claude Roger-Marx*
ENCYCLOPAEDIA OF MODERN ARCHITECTURE   edited by *Wolfgang Pehnt*
A CONCISE HISTORY OF BALLET   *F. Reyna*
A CONCISE HISTORY OF PHOTOGRAPHY   *Helmut and Alison Gernsheim*

Details of paperback editions of this series can be obtained from your bookseller

THAMES AND HUDSON 30 Bloomsbury Street, London, W.C.1

KING ALFRED'S COLLEGE
LIBRARY